LATIN AMERICAN HISTORICAL DICTIONARIES SERIES

Edited by A. Curtis Wilgus

1. *Guatemala,* by Richard E. Moore, rev. ed. 1973.
2. *Panama,* by Basil C. & Anne K. Hedrick. 1970.
3. *Venezuela,* by Donna Keyse & G. A. Rudolph. 1971.
4. *Bolivia,* by Dwight B. Heath. 1972.
5. *El Salvador,* by Philip F. Flemion. 1972.
6. *Nicaragua,* by Harvey K. Meyer. 1972.
7. *Chile,* by Salvatore Bizzarro. 1972.
8. *Paraguay,* by Charles J. Kolinski. 1973.
9. *Puerto Rico and the U. S. Virgin Islands,* by Kenneth R. Farr. 1973.
10. *Ecuador,* by Albert W. Bork and Georg Maier. 1973.

Historical Dictionary of Puerto Rico and the U.S. Virgin Islands

by

Kenneth R. Farr

Latin American Historical Dictionaries, No. 9

The Scarecrow Press, Inc.
Metuchen, N.J. 1973

Library of Congress Cataloging in Publication Data

Farr, Kenneth R
Historical dictionary of Puerto Rico and the U. S.
Virgin Islands.

(Latin American historical dictionaries, no. 9)
Bibliography: p.
1. Puerto Rico--Dictionaries and encyclopedias.
2. Virgin Islands of the United States--Dictionaries
and encyclopedias. I. Title.
F1954.F37 917.29'003 73-7603
ISBN 0-8108-0670-3

EDITOR'S FOREWORD

Puerto Rico, and to a much lesser degree the Virgin Islands, underwent a traumatic experience when they became a part of the United States political system. For the Puerto Ricans it proved at first to be more of a cultural shock than a political one. Following only a few months of war, they found themselves, after 400 years, separated from the mother country Spain and thrust into the alien arms of the United States. Suddenly they were confronted with another language, Anglo-Saxon culture, a different way of thinking and living, and strange political practices. For political leaders and intellectuals this was a "moment of truth." Some expressed fear of a "progressive cultural erosion" or a "cultural vacuum," which would have to be counteracted by a "period of identity" with the past. Some leaders sought to develop new political and cultural characteristics, first as a bridge between the old and the new, and then as new and separate accomplishments. This slow transition must be appreciated in order to understand Puerto Rico's recent political, economic and cultural history. Even today traces of Spanish colonial characteristics remain although political leaders in recent years have tried to modify and redirect many of these traits through vigorous actions to accomplish economic changes ("Operation Bootstrap"), social reforms, and cultural awareness. Of these facts and others the compiler of this volume is fully cognizant, and he has achieved a balanced treatment of both Puerto Rico and the Virgin Islands.

Dr. Kenneth R. Farr first became interested in Puerto Rico while enrolled at Valparaiso University in Indiana as an undergraduate student. There he was fortunate to have the opportunity of attending a seminar on the Caribbean on the San Germán campus of the Inter-American University of Puerto Rico. This gave him a first-hand view of the Island's history, people, problems and environment. This brief visit to the Caribbean led to a determination to specialize in Latin American studies. To accomplish this objective, he entered the University of Florida where he obtained a master's degree in the School of Inter-American Studies. His thesis dealt with the role of Luis Muñoz Marín in the development of the Popular Democratic Party in Puerto Rico. From Gainesville, he returned to the Island and began to teach at the University of Puerto Rico at Mayagüez. But this experience soon showed that he needed to know still more about Latin America, and he returned to the Mainland and entered Tulane University as a graduate in political science on a National Defense Fellowship. In 1971 he was awarded the Ph.D. degree with a dissertation concerned with the problems of institutionalizing political parties using the Popular Party of Puerto Rico as a case study. Fortunately for the students of the Island's political life this work is being published by the Inter-American University of Puerto Rico Press. Another product of his Puerto Rican studies is a chapter on comparative politics in the forthcoming book entitled, Introducción a las ciences sociales, edited by Dr. Eneida Rivero, and Dr. Baldomero Cores.

After completing his doctoral work, Kenneth returned to Mayagüez to continue his teaching, while at the same time he served as coordinator of political science from 1971-1973. Meanwhile, he has traveled in Latin America, lectured occasionally, served as an analyst and consultant to the Office of the Governor of Puerto Rico in the Citizen Feedback Project, and finds time to enjoy his family, a wife born in Ecuador and a small child.

A. Curtis Wilgus
Emeritus Director
School of Inter-American Studies
University of Florida

INTRODUCTION

When using this dictionary it is well to keep in mind the words of the series general editor, A. Curtis Wilgus, expressed in the Foreword to another volume:

> The assignment given to the compilers of the Historical Dictionaries was to select arbitrarily material for inclusion which was logical and justifiable, as well as comprehensive, so that each resulting volume would constitute a helpful, balanced, but not exhaustive guide and ready reference to pertinent topics....

This dictionary, then, is in no sense an encyclopedia, but is intended to be a guide and source book to provide factual data on persons, events, historically significant places, geographical and political subdivisions, and a sprinkling of pertinent definitions of terms.

A work of this type on Puerto Rico and the U.S. Virgin Islands seems especially appropriate at this time, both for the historical scholar and the layman. In the United States there has been an awakening interest in these uniquely affiliated political units. The creation of various Puerto Rican studies programs in the U.S. is one manifestation of this interest. Since both Puerto Rico and the Virgin Islands were long under Spanish and Danish rule, a consolidation of important data for that period is of particular usefulness.

The author has lived in Puerto Rico for six of the past eight years, carrying out extensive research on its politics. Frequent trips to the neighboring Virgin Islands were made to gather data on those islands. The Dictionary is divided into two sections; Puerto Rico, and the U.S. Virgin Islands. The much shorter colonial history, and the lesser size and population, are the major reasons why the section on the Virgin Islands is much shorter. Hopefully, the scholar and friend of the Virgin Islands will not be disappointed by this decision.

The entries are alphabetical, with extensive cross-references to related topics, abbreviations and pseudonyms. Spanish articles "el, los, la, las" are not considered in this ordering. For example, "El Antillano" is listed under "A."

Many historical events have been listed under the persons most involved in them, since it is really people which give meaning to events. Geographical entries include all the municipios in the case of Puerto Rico, and the major cities in the case of the Virgin Islands. Population and area figures are based on the official U.S. Census of 1970. It should be noted that these official figures have been highly questioned by Virgin Island authorities as being far too low.

For both Puerto Rico and the Virgin Islands a complete list of all governors (including acting governors), from the first until the present is given. The difficulty in obtaining an accurate list is formidable, since even primary sources are not in agreement. The period 1508-1511 in Puerto Rico is especially confusing, while in the Virgin Islands there were for a time two governors, one on St. Croix and another on St. Thomas. A careful attempt at complete accuracy for all dates has been made. However, the reader is cautioned again that even the primary sources, along with some of the most noted historians, are often in conflict.

An extensive bibliography is provided for the reader's more exhaustive investigation. In addition, since the format of this dictionary series does not include footnoting, it would be useful to point out those works most helpful in preparing this dictionary and which could be valuable for further research. The complete citation for all of them is found in the bibliography. On Puerto Rico the following were drawn upon extensively: Coll y Toste, Boletín histórico de Puerto Rico; Rivera de Alvarez, Diccionario de literatura puertorriqueña; Rives Tovar, Enciclopedia puertorriqueña ilustrada; and Hostos, Tesauro historico. For the Virgin Islands, refer to: Westergaard, The Danish West Indies under Company Rule; Seaman, The Virgin Islands Dictionary; Reid, Bibliography of the Virgin Islands of the United States; and the Von Scholten Collection of the Virgin Islands Public Library, St. Thomas, Virgin Islands.

The author wishes to acknowledge the assistance of various persons and institutions. Enid Baa and her assistant

Mrs. Lindquist of the Virgin Islands Public Library were most helpful to me, as was Mr. Henry Nieves, librarian at the University of Puerto Rico, Mayagüez. Mr. George Seaman generously gave me permission to quote several words from his Virgin Islands Dictionary. The University of Puerto Rico, Mayagüez, where I am a professor of political science, graciously provided funds for travel to carry out research. Special thanks goes out to my "compañero" Germán Delgado, professor of Puerto Rican history. He tediously read much of the manuscript, offering many helpful comments. Finally, a word of thanks is in order to my wife, Maria, since she did much of the typing of the manuscript.

Dr. Kenneth R. Farr
University of Puerto Rico, Mayagüez
December 1972

HISTORICAL DICTIONARY OF PUERTO RICO

- A -

ABAD, JOSE RAMON, c1850-1912. Born in Catalonia, Spain, he became a prominent journalist after emigrating to Puerto Rico at an early age. He strongly defended Puerto Rican liberties.

ABAY BENITEZ, JUAN, 1876-1901. Poet and novelist of a romantic bent.

ABBAD Y LASIERRA, FRAY IÑIGO, 1737-1830. A Benedictine monk, Abbad had gone to Puerto Rico in 1772. He was later commissioned to gather documented information as the basis for a history of the island. His Historia was first published in Madrid in 1788. While the work often lacks historical accuracy, it represents the fundamental historical account of the 18th century, relating much important data concerning the 16th and 17th centuries as well.

ABERCROMBY, SIR RALPH, 1734-1801. A British military official, whose command restored discipline and prestige to the British Army at the turn of the 18th century. He led the siege on San Juan in 1797, lasting from April 17-March 2. The attack swept across the city and against its fortifications, but Governor de Castro refused to surrender El Morro fortress. The English finally withdrew. See also MARTINEZ DE ANDINO, VICENTE.

ABRIL Y OSTALO, MARIANO, 1861-1935. Journalist, poet and writer. His liberal ideas were expressed in the newspaper La Democracia and as a legislator. In 1931 he became the Official Historian of Puerto Rico.

ACABE. A festive occasion with dancing, celebrated by the coffee harvesters and other workers on the coffee plantation at the conclusion of the annual harvest.

ACADEMIA ANTILLANA DE LA LENGUA. A language academy founded in San Juan in 1916 by José de Diego. Its founding reflected the concern among intellectual circles for preserving Hispanic culture in the face of americanization. Besides de Diego, other prominent literary and political figures of the period held posts in the Academy, including Coll y Toste and Fernández Juncos.

ACADEMIA PUERTORRIQUEÑA DE LA LENGUA ESPAÑOLA. The Spanish Language Academy was inaugurated April 1, 1955, as the result of an agreement by the Congress of Spanish Language Academies held in Mexico in 1952. Its purpose is the conservation and embellishment of the Spanish language and Hispanic culture.

ACADEMIA REAL DE BUENAS LETRAS. A literary, educational and cultural organization which began functioning July 9, 1850. By order of Marqués de la Perzuela, the governor, it had the responsibility for supervision and inspection of the schools. It also sponsored the first literary contests and awarded teaching certificates. It ceased to exist in 1865.

ACEROLA. A small fruit similar to a cherry in shape, color and manner of growth. It is rich in vitamins but not grown on a commercial basis.

ACOSTA Y CALBO, EDUARDO EUGENIO, 1823-1868. Poet. He initiated the annual publication Almanaques Aguinaldos de Puerto Rico.

ACOSTA Y CALBO, JOSE JULIAN, 1825-1891. Noted historian, newspaper editor and abolitionist. With others of his fellow countrymen in Spain he organized, in 1851, a society dedicated to the collection of documents pertinent to Puerto Rican history. He was also a deputy to the Spanish Cortes (parliament).

ACUÑA, FRANCISCO DE PAULA, 1839-1929. Lawyer and public official. He held the posts of Alcalde Mayor of San Juan, President of the Sociedad Económica de Amigos del País, and Supreme Court Justice.

ADELANTADO DEL MAR. The title acquired by Juan Ponce de León, conquistador of Puerto Rico, upon his expedition to Florida in 1512. The title of Adelantado was given to the person to whom a maritime expedition was entrusted. It conceded beforehand the right to govern the lands that one might discover or conquer.

ADJUNTAS. Municipio near the center of the island. It was organized in 1815 when its population numbered about 3,200. Area: 66 square miles. Population: 18,691.

ADUAR. The name given to indigenous villages; a village inhabited by Indians.

AGIOTISMO. The black market.

AGRARIAN REFORM. In 1900 the U. S. Congress approved a resolution in conjunction with the Organic Act of that year, limiting to 500 acres the amount of land a corporation could possess. But the authorities in Puerto Rico did not enforce this rule and with the rapid rise of private U. S. investment in sugar cane, large American corporations arose. By 1940, some 50 corporations possessed 188,000 acres of land in violation of the law. A key part of the reformist platform of the Popular Democratic Party which won the election of 1940 was based on agrarian reform and enforcement of the 500 acres law. With the Popular Party victory of 1940, legislation creating a Land Authority and land reform provisions was approved. In the years that followed the reforms were carried out with only limited effectiveness. Since manufacturing is now the more important sector, large landholdings are controversial mainly due to the high price of land and speculation in available land.

AGRICULTURE. From Spanish colonial times until the 1950's, agriculture was the mainstay of economic activity, providing both the greatest number of jobs and also the most income. Industrialization has now surpassed agriculture, the latter accounting for 25% of net national income by 1970, compared to only 5% from agriculture. Whereas in 1940 some 45% of the labor force was employed in agriculture, by 1972 this had dropped below 10%. Nearly all farm products have been on the decline, especially sugar cane production. See also separate headings for various crops: sugar, coffee, tobacco, etc.

AGUADA. Place where ships can be provided with supply of water.

AGUADA. Municipio on west coast. Much evidence points

to the fact that Columbus first landed near here in 1493, although the actual site is bitterly disputed. It was among the first Spanish settlements on the island, founded in 1510, under the name Sotomayor. Area: 30 square miles. Population: 25, 658.

AGUADILLA. Municipio at the northwest tip of the island. Officially founded in 1775 with a population of some 1, 000. It has recently been an area of population and economic decline, partially due to the phase-out of a giant U. S. Air Force base, Ramey, located here. The cabecera is a port city, located on a hill-enclosed bay. Area: 36 square miles. Population 51, 355.

AGUAS BUENAS. Municipio in the east-central portion of the island. Formally a barrio of Caguas, it was established as a separate municipio in 1838, due to the efforts of Captain Francisco de Sales. Area: 30 square miles. Population: 18, 600.

AGUAYO Y ALDEA, NICOLAS, 1808-1878. A man of many talents, he rose through various governmental posts and also held various educational positions. He was a man of liberal ideas and he opposed slavery.

AGÜEYBANA. The head Indian chieftain in Puerto Rico when the Spaniards arrived to conquer and colonize under Juan Ponce de León's leadership. He resided near the present site of Guanica, where he and Ponce de León met and became good friends. After his death, however, relations between the Indians and Spaniards deteriorated, with an open rebellion occurring in 1511. See also INDIAN REBELLION.

AGÜEYBANA II (EL BRAVO). Younger brother of Taino Chieftain Agüeybana, who succeeded him at his death. In 1511 he led a revolt against the Spaniards. Although the Spaniards lost many lives, the uprising was put down and Agüeybana II was killed.

EL AGUILA. Ignacio Aguila, a celebrated bandit. He won fame by his incredible ability to escape jail. Finally ordered shot in 1848.

AGUINALDO. Typical Puerto Rican Christmas carols, with criollo music. The term originates from early colonial times when singing groups celebrating the holiday season went from house to house, asking for the "aguinaldo." At that time the aguinaldo was usually a drink, food, or even money.

AGUINALDO PUERTORRIQUEÑO. A collection of original prose and verse, significant because it was among the earliest literature indigenous to the island. The first of these was published in 1843, under the direction of Ignacio Guasp Cervera. It marked a point of departure in the history of Puerto Rican letters, the start of criollo litterature.

AIBONITO. Municipio in central Puerto Rico. Its cabecera is located on the Aibonito River. Originally settled in 1630 by Pedro Zorescoechea from Viscaya, Spain. It was designated a municipio in 1822. Industries include tobacco processing, diamond-cutting and clothing. Area: 31 square miles. Population: 20,044.

ALBIZU CAMPOS, PEDRO, 1891-1965. Militant independence leader. As head of the Nationalist Party in the 1930's he worked tirelessly on behalf of separation from the U. S. Under his leadership the nationalists carried out violent uprisings in the 1950's both in Washington and Puerto Rico. Following this he was arrested and imprisoned until shortly before his death in 1965. His charismatic image still rallies independence sympathizers. See also NATIONALIST REVOLUTION OF 1950.

ALBUM PUERTORRIQUEÑO. A collection of poetry edited in Barcelona by a group of Puerto Rican students in the 19th century. Copies of the Album arrived in San Juan in 1844. Since some of the verses were harsh criticisms of the tyrannical government they were nearly destroyed by the governor, General Rafael de Arístegui. One of the most inciteful of these poems was titled "El Salvaje," written by Manuel Alonso Pacheco. See also ALONSO PACHECO, MANUEL.

ALCABALA. The percentage of the price of an article sold which the seller had to remit as tax. In the 18th century this was 0.5% and in the 19th century it rose to 2%.

ALCALDE. The cabecera of every municipio is the site of the municipal government, consisting today of a mayor (alcalde) and municipal assembly. Mayors today ride the coattails of gubernatorial candidates with little power or following in their own right. In Spanish times, however, the mayor often played a decisive political role.

ALCALDE MAYOR. These were mayors with greater jurisdiction and authority than the ordinary alcaldes. First established by Alfonso VI in Toledo, Spain, this title later became generalized. In Puerto Rico this post was assigned to the heads of the seven administrative districts, called partidos, by royal order of 1831. Each partido was composed of several towns. The alcalde mayor exercised both civil and criminal jurisdiction and had some powers of inspection in economic affairs. Governor de la Torre outlined their powers in a document of 1832 called, Instrucciones a los Tenientes a Guerra y a los Alcaldes Mayores.

ALCALDES ORDINARIOS. Liberal system of government ordered by Charles V in 1537; it lasted until 1544. It was two mayors; one in San Juan, one in San Germán.

ALCAPURRIA. Popular fried food made from grated plantains, yuca, or yuatía (root vegetables), stuffed with meat.

ALDEA. "Village." Governor Dabán (1884-1887) had proposed to found an aldea in each municipal district, with the idea of concentrating the rural population. They were to be established with government assistance, donations and popular and corporation subscriptions. A constitution was also written in 1886, establishing central and local Aldea Governing Boards. The first such aldea established was Cerrote, in Las Marías municipio.

ALEGRIA, RICARDO A., 1921- . Director of the Institute of Puerto Rican Culture and author of numerous cultural and historical studies. He is noted for his efforts to revive the island's folklore and traditions.

ALEGRIA SANTOS, JOSE S., 1886-1965. Poet, writer and newspaperman, as well as lawyer. As a political leader he headed the Nationalist Party in its less militant early years. He defended independence and held legislative posts in both the Senate and House.

ALMOJARIFAZGO. The right to charge a duty or tariff on goods imported and exported. As early as 1511 the Spanish King gave orders regarding this to the authorities in Puerto Rico, setting the duty at 7.5% on goods brought from Spain.

ALMONEDA. To sell the right to the use of land, while the Crown kept title to the property. This practice was begun in the first decade of the 16th century.

ALOJA. A popular 18th-century beverage prepared with honey, sugar, and spice, usually added to aguardiente (home-made rum).

ALONSO CANSINO, GARCIA. He is credited with introducing the first pigs and goats into the island. He was on the boat which carried Vincente Yáñez Pinzón to Hispañola in 1505, from where the settlement of Puerto Rico was established. See also YAÑEZ PINZON, VINCENTE.

ALONSO PACHECO, MANUEL, 1822-1889. Poet, writer and physician. As a writer he often described the daily life and customs of Puerto Rico. His works are collected in the book, El Jibaro, described by one historian as the Puerto Rican equivalent of El Cid. See also ALBUM PUERTORRIQUEÑO.

ALONSO PINZON, MARTIN. One of Spain's greatest sailors, he accompanied Columbus on the first voyage to America as captain of the "Pinta." Some historians say he deserves more credit for the voyage and even suggest he may have been the first European to have seen Puerto Rico, on the 1492 voyage, rather than Columbus, on the second voyage in 1493. This supposedly occurred during his six-week desertion of Columbus' expedition, but is difficult to corroborate.

ALVAREZ MARRERO, FRANCISCO, 1847-1888. Poet, dramatist and journalist.

AMEZQUITA Y QUIJANO, JUAN, 1598-1650. Little is known about this Spanish military captain, but he is notorious due to his role in the heroic defense of the El Morro fortress during the Dutch attack of 1625. At that time he was governor of El Morro and apparently engaged in hand-to-hand battle with the leader of the Dutch,

Bowdoin Hendrick, resulting in the latter's death the following year.

AMY, FRANCISCO J., 1837-1912. A Puerto Rican writer who studied and lived in the United States, later becoming a citizen there. He wrote and published in both Spanish and English. He was named official translator by the Americans after the takeover of the island in 1898. He defended annexation of the island to the U. S.

AÑASCO. Municipio on the west coast. It takes its name from a lieutenant of Juan Ponce de León, Luis de Añasco, its founder. It officially became recognized as a town in 1728, but its port was used for clandestine trade with Jamaica and Curacao in the 17th century. Agriculture continues to be the leading source of income here, with sugar cane the leading crop. Area: 40 square miles. Population: 19, 416.

ANDINO, JOSE DE, 1751-1835. The island's first newspaperman, as the editor of the Diario Económico de Puerto Rico, the first privately published newspaper (1814-1815). He also held the post of Minister of the Treasury and was a defender of constitutional liberalism.

ANDINO, JULIAN DE, 1845-1920. Virtuoso violinist and composer. He wrote more than 50 "danzas", a popular 19th-century music form.

ANGLERIA, PEDRO MARTIR DE [Pietro Martire d'Anghiera], ca. 1457-1526. One of the early, lesser known chroniclers of the Spanish conquest in America. As an Italian humanist resident in Spain he gained important friendships. He became a member of the Council of the Indies, thus gaining access to the official documents related to the discovery and conquest. His writings include data on the discovery of Puerto Rico.

EL ANTILLANO (pseudonym) see BETANCES, RAMON EMERITO

APONTE, JOSE AGUSTIN, ?-1910. A writer, poet and orator of humble origin, he in fact earned his living as a barber.

ARCE, DIEGO. A 16th-century Spanish official in Puerto

Rico. By royal cédula of May, 1510, he was named the king's "Veedor." This post was a treasury official who watched over the mining and minting of gold and silver. He also became a regidor, or councilman, of the Caparra municipio. In this position he recommended to the king in 1517 that the capital be moved from Caparra to its present site on the islet of San Juan. This transfer took place in 1521.

ARCE DE VASQUEZ, MARGOT, 1904- . Among the most noteworthy contemporary literary critics. Her essays have evaluated many leading poets both in Puerto Rico and throughout the Americas.

ARECIBO. Municipio midway along the north coast. Its name is derived from a Taino Indian chieftain. One of the oldest towns on the island, it was settled by the Spanish in 1556, the town being chartered in 1616. It was successfully defended when the English laid siege to the town August 5, 1702. Its cabecera is located along the Río Grande River. It is one of the island's principal cities, while the surrounding area is a center for sugar growing and rum production. Area: 127 square miles. Population: 73, 468.

AREYTO. Indian festivals held in celebration of some memorable event past or present. Lasting several days, the festivals included uninhibited dancing, singing and drinking, as well as the relating of important events such as the death of a Spaniard. Lacking a written language, the Indians used the areytos as a means of orally transmitting historical and religious events. It was thus a kind of indigenous "oral epic."

"AREYTO": Sociedad Dramática de Teatro Popular. A popular theater and dramatic society founded in 1940 by Emilio S. Belaval under the auspices of the Ateneo Puertorriqueño. It was composed of actors and authors whose essential purpose was to keep alive the enthusiasm for a national theater. This theater group gave a notable impulse to contemporary theater, but has since been dissolved. Today, however, the Areyto is operating as a folk dancing troupe.

ARIZMENDI, JUAN ALEJO DE, 1757/60-1814. Named Bishop of the Catholic Church in 1803, Alejo became the first Puerto Rican to occupy such a high ecclesiastical post. He was a prelate of liberal persuasion, likeable, erudite and charitable to the poor.

ARQUEO DE CAJA. The term is used to denote the change in sovereignty over Puerto Rico in 1898, from Spain to the United States.

ARRELDE. A measure of weight that was used principally by butchers and meat markets. It is the equivalent of four pounds. It is probably Arabic in origin, from the word arratl, meaning pound.

ARRILLAGA ROQUE, JUAN, 1866-1907. In addition to being a noted politician, he was a writer, journalist, dramatist and pharmacist. He gained distinction for his courageous actions in the face of harsh persecutions of liberals by Governor Palacios in 1887. In 1889 he was President of the Partido Autonomista. See also EL COMPONTE.

ARRIMADO. A share-cropper. A person who has received the concession to use a piece of land for his house and crops. He plants a crop which is partly for himself and partly for the owner.

ARROYO. Small municipio on the southeast coast. Founded in 1855 as a port for Guayama, of which it had been a barrio. Its cabecera, located on the Caribbean, was captured by the American warship Gloucester during the Spanish-American War. Area: 15 square miles. Population: 13, 033.

ARUACAS. The Arawak Indian group which inhabited the Greater Antilles. They were noted for their peaceful nature in contrast to the fierce Carib Indians of the nearby Lesser Antilles, which frequently attacked them and later the Spaniards. The Arawaks were an agricultural people, with the yuca plant being their chief crop. The Taino Indians of Puerto Rico were a type of Arawak. See also TAINO INDIANS.

ASENJO Y ARTEAGA, FEDERICO, 1831-1893. An educator, economist, writer and journalist.

ASHFORD, BAILEY K., 1873-1934. A North American doctor who went to Puerto Rico in 1898. He is noted for his discovery of the parasite which was the cause of persistent anemia on the island.

ASOPAO. A criollo dish, made from a rice base. Similar to a thick soup or stew, it generally contains either seafood or chicken.

ATENEO PUERTORRIQUEÑO. Founded on June 29, 1876, chiefly due to the efforts of Manuel Elzaburu. Its avowed purpose is to conserve and enrich Puerto Rican culture, and to serve as an organization to promote the arts, science, literature and education. The Ateneo carries out publications, expositions and theater, as well as maintaining a library.

AUDIENCIA. A judicial, consultative and administrative body which also had the authority to govern a territory in the absence of other functionaries. It served as the highest court of appeal within a given district of the colonial empire of Spain. As a court it tried both civil and criminal cases, it heard complaints of individuals against the highest authorities, and was charged with protecting the interests of the Indians.

AUDIENCIA REAL DE LA ESPAÑOLA. In 1511 this Audiencia was established in Santo Domingo (Dominican Republic). It served as the court of appeals for the sentences dictated by the Governors of Puerto Rico. When the colony later obtained the status of capitanía general, this audiencia lost some of its jurisdictional rights. It was moved to Cuba in 1797.

AUDIENCIA REAL TERRITORIAL DE PUERTO RICO. This audiencia was established by royal decree of 1815. Its jurisdiction was separated from the Audiencia de Puerto Principe in Cuba in 1831. The tribunal was presided over by the capitán general.

AYALA Y TOMAS, ESTEBAN DE, 1778-1838. He held several administrative posts and helped obtain the reestablishment of elective municipal councils for Puerto Rico. Most noted however as the valuable assistant to Ramón Power, Puerto Rico's outstanding deputy to the Spanish Cortes.

AYERRA Y SANTA MARIA, FRANCISCO, 1630-1708. Priest and poet. As a priest he studied canon law in Mexico and held several ecclesiastical posts. He published many works of poetry at the end of the 17th century, for which some historians cite him as the first Puerto Rican poet. His most notable work was the sonnet, Gongorist in style.

AYESA Y LAMI, GABRIEL, 1763-1840. An early liberal and defender of the Spanish Constitution of 1812. Elected as a deputy to the Cortes in 1814 he never took office, since the Constitution was nullified when Ferdinand VII declared himself absolute.

AYMAMON. One of the local chieftains, caciques, of the Taino Indians when Ponce de León arrived to conquer the island in 1508.

AYUNTAMIENTO. Municipal government organization established for the colonies. The first to be set up in Puerto Rico was at Caparra, 1511. See also CABILDO.

- B -

BALBUENA, BERNARDO DE, 1568?-1627. Spanish-born priest and man of letters who was named Bishop of Puerto Rico in 1619. Arriving at this post in 1623, he served until his death in 1627. He was a distinguished Baroque poet of the time. His initiation of a literary scholarly development on the island was halted abruptly when his works and library were destroyed by the Dutch assault on San Juan in 1625.

BALDORIOTY DE CASTRO, ROMAN, 1822-1889. Among the island's leading political and literary figures of the 19th century. Through his writings Puerto Rican coffee gained a world reputation in the 1860's. He defended liberalization of the colonial regime and abolition of slavery. As a deputy to the Cortes in 1870 he became distinguished as an orator and defender of colonial rights. His strong stance in favor of autonomy led to persecutions, imprisonment and exile at the hands of the Spanish authorities.

BANDO DE POLICIA Y BUEN GOBIERNO DE 1824. This was an extensive law issued by Governor Miguel de la Torre in late December 1823 and published in early 1824. It was one of the basic canons of Spanish colonial law for Puerto Rico. Its 66 articles described regulations and punishments in numerous fields, including behavior, gambling, arms, construction, commerce, and travel. See also LOS BANDOS.

LOS BANDOS. The collection of laws by which Puerto Rico was governed until 1868 was known as "los bandos."

BANEQUE, OR BANBEQUE. An Indian word referring to a rich, luxurious island which the natives had described to Columbus on his first voyage. The word appears several times in Columbus' diary, and for a while it was much sought after. Since it was described as lying to the east of Santo Domingo, some historians believe the island referred to was Puerto Rico.

BARBOSA, JOSE CELSO, 1857-1921. Physician, educator and political leader. He began his political career in 1883 by joining the Liberal Party. He later split with Luis Muñoz Rivera by insisting on his own criteria for an autonomous government. Barbosa then helped to form the Orthodox Liberal Party in 1897. Upon the U. S. takeover in 1898, Barbosa became a fervent defender of Federal Statehood. He founded the Republican Party in 1900. He held many posts on the Executive Council established under the First Organic Act of 1900.

BARCELO, ANTONIO R., 1868-1938. Political leader, orator and journalist. He held several high elective offices, including President of the Senate, 1917-1930. He headed both the Union Party (1916-1932), and the Liberal Party (1932-1938).

BARCELONETA. Municipio along the north coast. The name is Catalonian in origin, a diminutive of Barcelona. The municipio was officially established in 1881. Area: 34 square miles. Population: 20, 792.

BARRANQUITAS. Municipio lying in the mountains of central Puerto Rico. It attained town status under the Spaniards in 1804 and is noted as the birthplace of two of the island's most prominent figures, Luis Muñoz Rivera and his son, Luis Muñoz Marín. Area: 33 square miles. Population: 20, 118.

BARRIO. Neighborhood or precinct. Several rural barrios surround the cabecera (administrative center) of each municipio, while the urban centers are also divided into various urban barrios.

BARROS see OROCOVIS

BASTIDAS, RODRIGO DE, 1498-1570. Spanish cleric who became Bishop of Puerto Rico and later Archbishop of Santo Domingo. He wrote and travelled widely, doing much of his work in Puerto Rico. In 1533 he sought to end the Inquisition. He put into effect the royal decree of 1542 giving freedom to the Indians. His father was a noted conquistador who accompanied Balboa to Panama and was also noted for befriending the Indians.

BATATA. Sweet potato indigenous to the island. It was cultivated from the earliest colonization and continues to be a popular food.

BATEY. A word of jíbaro (peasant) usage, meaning the yard in front of his country dwelling.

BATEY. A newspaper previously published by the Popular Democratic Party.

BAYAMON. Urban municipio adjacent to San Juan. Until 1772 it was a barrio of Guaynabo. In recent years it has been among the most rapidly growing areas of population, commerce and industry and serves as a "bedroom suburb" of San Juan. Area: 44 square miles. Population: 156, 192.

BELAND, GUILLERMO. The inventor of a gas lighting system which was purchased by the municipality of San Juan in 1831. The liquid fuel was a mixture of turpentine and aguardiente.

BENDITO. An interjection of common usage. Although religious in origin it is generally used in everyday conversation, indicating pleading, commiseration or pity. "¡Ay Bendito!" is a variant often used.

BENITEZ, JAIME, 1908- . Educator, essayist and speaker of hemisphere renown. President of the University of Puerto Rico from 1942-1971, when he was dismissed amid much controversy. In 1972 he was elected the Resident Commissioner to Washington.

BENITEZ, MARIA BIBIANA, 1783-1873. Puerto Rico's first woman poet. She used a mixture of forms; decima, classical sonnets and others, but most commonly romantic verse.

BENITEZ Y DE ARCE, ALEJANDRINA, 1819-1879. In chronological order the second woman poet of the island, but considered the outstanding poetic figure during 1843-1879 period.

BERLANGA, TOMAS DE. A Spanish friar who is credited with introducing the plantain from Santo Domingo in 1516. He also was known as a defender of Indian rights.

BERRIOS MARTINEZ, RUBEN A., 1939- . Militant young President of the Puerto Rico Independence Party. Under his leadership the party has taken a strong ideological stand in favor of independence with socialism, and the use of non-violent civil disobedience. See also PARTIDO INDEPENDENTISTA PUERTORRIQUEÑO.

BETANCES, RAMON EMERITO, 1827-1898. Physician, writer and political activist. Among the foremost opponents of the Spanish colonial regime, and a noted abolitionist. In addition to separation from Spain he envisioned the creation of an independent Antillian Confederation, created out of the West Indian colonies. His liberalism led to persecution and flight to other Caribbean territories and later to Europe, where he spent the last 20 years of his life. A versatile writer, he wrote prose and verse in both Spanish and French. He died as a pauper in France.

BIMINI. Ancient name for the State of Florida. Discovered in 1512 by Juan Ponce de León, shortly after leaving his post of Governor of Puerto Rico.

BLANCO, TOMAS, 1900- . Novelist, historian and newspaperman. Especially noted for his historical works, such as Prontuario histórico de Puerto Rico.

BLANCO Y SOSA, JULIAN E., 1830-1905. A distinguished writer, journalist, and politician. In 1871 he was a deputy to the Spanish Cortes. He devoted much energy and writing to efforts at liberalizing the colonial regime. His political ideals caused him both persecution and exile.

BOHIO. Jíbaro terminology; the peasant's humble, cabin-like home in the rural countryside.

BOLITA. The clandestine lottery, as opposed to the official government-operated weekly lottery. See also LOTERIA.

BOLIVAR, SIMON, 1783-1830. The world-renowned soldier-statesman who was the liberator of six Latin American Republics. Following his successes against the Spanish in Venezuela rumors circulated in Puerto Rico about his intention of liberating the island, as he had once promised to do. Actual Venezuelan expeditions attempted landings, but were turned back. In 1816, following an initial loss to Spanish forces, Bolívar had touched ashore at Vieques, Puerto Rico, repairing his ship and taking on supplies. See also VENEZUELA'S INTERVENTION.

BOMBA. A large drum, especially used during Christmas season for typical music.

BOMBA. A popular dance of African origin, accompanied by singing.

BONILLA Y TORRES, JOSE ANTONIO, 1770-1855. Franciscan priest and eloquent defender of justice and constitutionalism. He clashed with the bishop over abuses in charging for marriages and wills, and was deported to Spain. In Spain he won his case and returned to defend the new law against such practices.

BORICUA OR BORINCANO. Synonym for a Puerto Rican.

BORINQUEÑO. Poetic, elevated synonym for a Puerto Rican. "El Borinqueño" is also the title of Puerto Rico's national anthem.

BORIQUEN. The primitive Indian name for Puerto Rico. It meant the "land of the valiant one." The Spaniards soon changed the pronunciation to Borínquén, by which it is still popularly known. The official name given to the island by Columbus was San Juan Bautista, probably in honor of Prince John, son and heir of the Catholic Kings of Spain. Early in the colonial period a confusion of names with that of the capital city, Puerto Rico, occurred and the names became reversed.

BOROCOCO Y ZAPATEADOS. Rustic country dances popular in the first half of the 19th century.

BOTICA. Pharmacy or apothecary. The island's first pharmacy was opened by the royal order of June 17, 1767, in San Juan adjacent to the Military Hospital.

BOZALES. Negro slaves.

BRACETTI, MARIANA, c1840-? Patriotic heroine of the short-lived Grito de Lares revolt against Spain in 1868. She sewed the flag used by the rebel forces. See also GRITO DE LARES.

BRAU, SALVADOR, 1842-1912. Distinguished historian, writer and journalist. He was the Official Historian of Puerto Rico until his death.

BRUCKMAN, MATHIAS. A North American who was one of the leading officers in the independence revolt at Lares, September 23, 1868. One week after the initial capture of Lares, Bruckman was killed by Spanish forces. See also GRITO DE LARES.

BUSCAGLIA, JOSE, 1938- . Puerto Rico's leading sculptor.

BUYL, BERNAL (or Bernardo). A monk who officiated at the first Catholic mass held in the West Indies in 1494.

- C -

CABALLERIA. A Spanish agrarian measurement. In Puerto Rico a caballería of land is equal to 200 square cuerdas. A cuerda is the most common unit of land measurement today and equals 4, 000 square meters, or a little less than one acre.

CABECERA. The governmental administrative center of each municipio. The principal town within each municipio which has the same name as the municipio.

CABILDO. Municipal organization. Under Spanish administration there were both secular and ecclesiastical cabildos. Ponce de León established the first secular cabildo at Caparra. While the cabildo members were generally named by the Crown and not of popular origin, they did possess rights and privileges which the king respected. A Papal Bull issued in Rome August 8, 1511, established the Diocese of Puerto Rico, thus constituting the ecclesiastical cabildo and the organization of the cathedral shortly thereafter.

CABO ROJO. Municipio in the southwest. Founded by virtue of a decree of 1771, by Col. Miguel de Musas. It is noted for its fine beaches, fishing villages and sugar cane. Area: 72 square miles. Population: 26, 060.

CAGUAS. Municipio to the south of San Juan. The town was ordered founded in 1774 and constituted in 1775. The name comes from the Indian cacique Caguax, who resided near here. Today's chief economic activities include cattle raising, sugar cane and tobacco crops and cigar factories. Area: 58 square miles. Population: 95, 661.

CAMPBELL BILL. This was an unsuccessful legislative bill authored by Congressmen Philip P. Campbell in the 1922 U. S. Congress. It proposed the creation of a political status for Puerto Rico similar to the Commonwealth which was established in 1952.

CAMPECHE, JOSE, 1752-1809. The first known Puerto Rican painter. He mainly did religious themes. An artist of natural vocation, lacking formal training until later years.

CAMUY. Municipio on the northwest coast. It became a municipio in 1807 and derived its name from an Indian word. The chief crop is sugar cane, with much rum produced in the area. Area: 46 square miles. Population: 19, 922.

CANALES, NEMESIO R., 1878-1923. Lawyer, politician, newspaperman, and literary humorist.

CANARY ISLANDS. A Spanish archipelago less than 100 miles off the northwest coast of Africa. After establishment of Spanish sovereignty in the late 15th century they became an important base for Columbus' departures. Emigration from these islands to Puerto Rico was first stimulated by a royal cédula of April 11, 1688, which granted the emigrants land in Puerto Rico. These emigrants settled the towns of Toa Alta in 1813 and Vega Alta and Trujillo Alto in 1814. The

Canary Islands were also the source of the first sugar cane introduced into the Americas.

CANGREJOS, SAN MATEO DE. The early colonial name of Santurce, which is now a barrio of San Juan and center of the commercial district. It was founded formally in 1760 by slaves escaped from other islands in the Caribbean.

CAÑITA. Clandestine-made rum. Also known as petriche.

CANOVANAS. Municipio southeast of San Juan. Its name is derived from a Taino chieftain, Canóbana. Until the 1970's it was a barrio of Loiza municipio to the north.

CAPARRA. The first settlement in Puerto Rico and among the oldest in the New World. The name Caparra was chosen by Nicolás Ovando, Governor of the Indies, but later ordered changed to Puerto Rico by the king. It was founded in late 1508 by Juan Ponce de León, in the high area overlooking the present capital city. Ponce soon returned to Santo Domingo to report his settlement to Governor Ovando and seek recruits for a permanent colony. Ponce then returned in 1509 as Governor. Uniquely, he immediately brought his family with him to Caparra, being the only one of the noted conquistadores to do this. The early colonists were unhappy with the Caparra site, complaining of disease, inaccessibility, and the long distance from the port. The capital of the colony was thus moved across the bay to the present site of San Juan, on an islet, in 1521.

CAPITACION. A type of head tax paid by slave owners to keep the right to own slaves.

CAPITAN GENERAL. At one time the highest rank in the Spanish military, equivalent to field marshal. The title was also conferred on non-military nobles, however. One of the smaller categories of political administrative units established by Spain was known as the Capitanía General. Puerto Rico acquired this status in 1643. The head of the government then became the Capitán General. Even prior to its creation several governors of the island used this title, beginning with Diego de Menéndez Valdés in 1582.

CAPITULACIONES. Contracts, pacts or covenants. In Spanish law this term may refer to different types of contracts, from marriage to international agreements. In Puerto Rican history the capitulaciones between Ovando, Governor of the Indies, and Juan Ponce de León, were noteworthy. The first capitulación issued to Ponce in 1508 authorized the exploration of Puerto Rico. The second, issued after Ponce's initial report, authorized the colonization of the island in 1509. A legal battle between Ponce and Diego Columbus over this capitulación then ensued in which Columbus (Christopher's son), finally won. See also PONCE DE LEON, JUAN; COLUMBUS, DIEGO.

CARBONELL, SALVADOR. Physician and leader in the Partido Liberal Reformista. He was a staunch liberal but never agreed to conspire against Spain. The Spanish authorities suspected him, however, and he was one of those arrested after the Grito de Lares uprising in 1868. In 1898 he was named to the cabinet established by the Autonomous Charter granted by Spain.

CARDONA, FRANCISCO DE. First treasurer of Puerto Rico. During the early colonial period this post was subject to the Treasurer of the Indies, Miguel de Pasamonte.

CARIBBEAN COMMISSION. An international organization which existed from 1946-1961, when it became the Caribbean Organization. Its members included the metropolitan states with Caribbean possessions (U. S., England, France, and Holland); thus the U. S. was a member because of its ties with Puerto Rico and the Virgin Islands. The purpose of the organization was avowedly to bring greater cooperation and integration to the area.

CARIBBEAN ORGANIZATION. A short lived international organization aimed at Caribbean integration. It was an out-growth of the Caribbean Commission. Significantly, it was the first international body of which most of the members, like Puerto Rico, were not sovereign independent nations. Its headquarters were located in San Juan for a time. The withdrawal of the organization's biggest members, Jamaica and Trinidad, when they gained independence in 1962, spelled the beginning of the end. Continuing political, budget and constitutional problems brought the final demise of the organization when its biggest financial contributor, Puerto Rico, withdrew in 1964.

CARIMBO. The mark, or official stamp, branded on each African slave legally entered into the country. The iron used for making this mark was also known as the carimbo. This practice was abolished by a royal order of November 4, 1784. However, a tax on slaves continued to be collected until February 1789, when free commerce of slaves was allowed. See also SLAVERY.

CAROLINA. A municipio which today has become part of the urban San Juan area to the west. In 1854 the creation of a new town on the present site was authorized, and in 1857 its founding was ordered by Captain Lorenzo Vizcarrondo. Area: 48 square miles. Population: 107, 643.

CARTA AUTONOMICA DE 1897. The Autonomous Charter was granted to Puerto Rico by Spain only a few months before the colony was taken over by the U. S. as a prize of the Spanish-American War. The Charter is often cited for its more generous autonomy and self-government provisions than were allowed under later U. S. legislation. Formally it provided an official recognition of existing representation in the Spanish parliament (Cortes) and authority of an insular legislature to legislate on internal affairs, including tariff and customs duties. Despite these provisions Spain did not relinquish in any sense her sovereignty over Puerto Rico. Further, the Spanish-appointed governor general retained extensive exclusive powers. Some observors feel that the Charter's concessions were not so much the result of efforts of liberal Puerto Rican statesmen like Luis Muñoz Rivera, but rather due to Spain's preoccupation with the rebellion in Cuba at this time, and the desire to convince Cuba of reform efforts.

CASA BLANCA [also, Casa Fuerte]. A fortress-type building overlooking San Juan harbor. It was constructed by García Troche, son-in-law of Juan Ponce de León, by authorization of a royal order of 1523. It is located adjacent to the later-constructed governor's palace, La Fortaleza. It was used by some of the governors and Ponce de León's heirs from 1530-1773. In 1779 it was purchased by the government in a state of deterioration. It has now been restored and continues to be used for offices of the Commonwealth government.

CASA DE CONTRATACION. Founded by Ferdinand and Isabella in January 1503 in Seville, Spain, it was the royal storehouse for all the gold coming from the Indies; however, it generally regulates movement to the Indies, issuing passports, etc.

CASABE [or Cazabe, or Casabi]. Name the Indians gave to their bread. It was made from the flour of the yuca plant. Yuca, a tuberous plant, was indigenous and became the first agricultural crop. The casabe bread was thin, waferlike in nature. It is rarely prepared today due to the lack of yuca and persons knowing this technique.

CASALS, PABLO, 1876- . World-renowned cellist. Casals was born in Spain of a Puerto Rican mother. Since the 1950's he has resided in Puerto Rico and organized the Festival Casals, an annual series of concerts, theater and ballet of high quality, sponsored by the Puerto Rican Institute of Culture.

CASAS, FRAY BARTOLOME DE LAS, c1470-1566. One of the best-known historians of the Spanish conquests. He first arrived on Hispañola in 1502. In his excellently documented work, Historia de las Indias, he describes the indigenous population of Boriquén, as well as the conquest and colonization of Puerto Rico. In 1535 he urged the king to send Negro slaves to replace the Indians which he staunchly defended. Some historians thus erroneously credit him with initiating slavery in the Americas. But this practice was well known in Spain and had been suggested for the Indies by the king himself and by Columbus many years earlier.

CASTELLANOS, JUAN DE, 1522-1605. Spanish poet noted for his composition, "Elegías de varones illustres de Indias," the longest poem in Spanish literature. Part of this poem is dedicated to exhalting the conquest of Boriquén. Castellanos is also the first poet to put into Spanish verse descriptive elements of the island's geography and history.

CASTILLO DE SAN FELIPE see EL MORRO

CATAÑO. Smallest municipio in Puerto Rico. Named after

a Spanish physician who arrived in 1569, Cataño was separated from Bayamón in 1927. Part of metropolitan San Juan, it is an area of concentrated industry and large slums. Area: 5 square miles. Population: 26, 459.

CATHOLIC UNIVERSITY OF PUERTO RICO. A co-educational, Roman Catholic university founded in 1948 at Ponce. It now has smaller campuses throughout the island and is accredited in the U. S. by the Middle States Association.

CAVES. The limestone base and karst topography found in parts of the island have provided an abundance of caves. Historically they were used by the indigenous inhabitants as dwellings and later as hideouts by pirates. Some of the better known sites are near Arecibo, Aguas Buenas, Loiza and Utuado.

CAYEY. Municipio nestled in the eastern mountains, founded in 1774. The chief crop is tobacco, with cigar factories an important offshoot. Coffee and mixed fruits are also cultivated. Area: 50 square miles. Population: 38, 432.

CEDULA DE GRACIA. A royal cédula of August 10, 1815. This promulgated a very significant law for the island's economic development. It decreed a 15-year exemption from various taxes, free trade with Spain, along with a low duty on trade with foreign countries, and permission for foreigners to settle in Puerto Rico. The settlers were also granted naturalization and the same rights as Spaniards after five years' residence. This act greatly stimulated the growth of population and capital investment from outside, since many were fleeing the independence movements in the Americas at this time. The flow of immigrants from Venezuela was so great, in fact, that Spain had to provide special financial aid to them.

CEIBA. Municipio at the eastern tip of the island. It was separated from Fajardo as an independent municipio in 1838. Area: 27 square miles. Population: 10, 312.

CELIS AGUILERA, JOSE DE, 1827-1893. Wealthy landowner who used his fortune to defend Puerto Rican rights. He was deported because of his political views but later, in 1873, was named deputy to the Cortes.

CEMIS. God-images commonly used in the religion of the indigenous Taino Indians. Some of these figures had the face of a human and the feet of a frog-like animal.

CENSUS OF PUERTO RICO. The Spanish established the first census by an order of 1776. The official census is now carried out by the U. S. Bureau of the Census, a federal agency. In the years between each dicennial census, the Puerto Rican Planning Board publishes periodic estimates. For 1970 the census showed a population of nearly 2. 75 millions, an increase of more than 340, 000 since 1960. Given the 3, 435 square mile area of the island (including smaller off-shore islands), this results in a high density of some 800 persons per square mile, compared with the 1966 world average of 57 per square mile.

CERON, JUAN. Second "governor" of Puerto Rico, although his official title was Alcalde Mayor. Cerón was involved in a dispute with Ponce de León and Diego Columbus over who had the right to name the governor of Puerto Rico. At one point, in 1509, Ponce had conceded the post to Cerón, whom Columbus had named Alcalde Mayor. But shortly thereafter an order from the king arrived granting the governor's title to Ponce. Ponce then had Cerón and his assistants arrested and sent to Spain. In the ensuing legal battles, Columbus won the right to name the governor, thus returning Cerón to his post and ousting once more Ponce de León in 1511. Cerón is credited with establishing the first "cabildo" or municipal council at San Germán, as well as the first grants of Indians, called repartimientos.

CERRO DE PUNTO. Highest peak on the island, located in the heart of the Cordillera Central, just south of the town of Jayuya. Its elevation is 1, 338 meters, or 4, 398 feet.

CHANCLETA. A word of popular usage in referring to a new-born baby girl. Also means woman, or female.

CHARDON, CARLOS E., 1897-1965. Doctor of science, agricultural engineer and researcher. His fame and achievements in the agricultural field were hemispheric.

He served as chancellor of the University of Puerto Rico, 1931-1936. He was a close associate of President Roosevelt's administration and one of the chief architects of Puerto Rico's equivalent of the New Deal.

CHARLES V, 1500-1558. Holy Roman Emperor and jointly the King of Spain under the title of Charles I. He insisted that the Indians be declared free, like any Spanish citizen, and that the encomienda system be abolished. In the 1540's he declared that pastures, rivers, and forests in Puerto Rico were part of the public domain. This measure prevented the land from being engulfed by private owners. However, he also promoted sugar cane development and authorized the importation of Negro slaves into the Antilles.

CHAVO. One United States cent, the penny. The term is also used in a generic sense to refer to money--"tiene chavo," he has money!

CHINA. The common, edible orange, which grows abundantly. In Puerto Rico, the more familiar Spanish word for orange, "naranja," refers to a bitter variety of orange used for cooking.

CHINCHORROS DE EMAJAGUA. The hammock used by the poor, rural folk of the island.

CIALES. Municipio. When founded in 1820 it was given the name Lacy (or Laci) after the Spanish Republican General. After Lacy was later declared a traitor the name was changed to Ciales. A long dispute with a neighboring barrio, Orocovis, over geographical boundary, lasted until 1880. Area: 66 square miles. Population: 15, 595.

CIDRA. Municipio in the east-central region, situated on a high plateau. Founded in 1809. Its name literally means cider, and comes from the fact that a German botanist supposedly planned to make cider from the apple trees planted in the vicinity of the town in the late 18th century. Area: 36 square miles. Population: 23, 892.

CLIFFORD, SIR GEORGE, 1558-1605. Third Earl of Cumberland and a British naval officer who succeeded in capturing San Juan in 1598. It was one of the only successful attacks on the El Morro fortress. After some 40 days of occupation he was forced to withdraw from the city, however, because of a severe outbreak of dysentery among his forces.

COAMO. Municipio in south central Puerto Rico. It was established as a religious community in 1579 by Fray Diego de Salamanca, and soon became noted for its thermal waters. In 1778 it was granted the cédula declaring it a "villa." At that time Coamo constituted one of the five district administrative centers of the island. Today's principal crop is coffee. Area: 77 square miles. Population: 26, 468.

COAT OF ARMS OF PUERTO RICO. The coat of arms, which is today the Official Seal, is the same one granted to the colony by King Ferdinand in 1511. It was the first coat of arms given to a colony in the New World. In the center is a white lamb embracing a red banner, kneeling upon a book, all of which is atop a green island--Puerto Rico. At the sides of the Seal are the letters F and I, for Ferdinand and Isabella, the King and Queen of Spain.

CODECA see CORPORACION DE DESARROLLO ECONOMICO DEL CARIBE

COFFEE. It was introduced from Haiti in 1736. By the end of the 19th century it became a principal crop, with large demand in Europe and a protected market in Spain. After the arrival of the U. S., coffee was not given special protection on the U. S. market as were sugar and tobacco. Consequently, production dropped drastically by the 1920's. Coffee is grown mainly in the moist, cool western mountain region (500 to 2, 000 feet elevation). It remains a major crop, although even the domestic demand is not met and it is not a major source of income.

COFRESI Y RAMIREZ DE ARELLANO, ROBERTO, 1791-1825. A legendary Puerto Rican pirate, born in Cabo Rojo. He began pirating activities in 1823. By 1825 he was captured near Patillas by the Spanish authorities and later shot at El Morro fortress.

COJIBA OR COJOBA. An Indian ceremony in which tobacco was inhaled through the nose.

COLL Y TOSTE, CAYETANO, 1850-1930. Politician, historian and poet. Noted for his editorship of the Boletín Histórico de Puerto Rico, an invaluable account of Puerto Rican history and culture. He also held several high administrative and elective posts, including that of Official Historian.

COLUMBUS, CHRISTOPHER, 1451?-1506. Discoverer of Puerto Rico on his second voyage to America in 1493. He is thought to have come ashore near the village of Aguada on the west coast, November 19, but there is much disagreement as to the site and even as to the date. The island, then called Boriquén by the Indians, was named by Columbus, Isla de San Juan Bautista (San Juan). Later the island took the name of its largest city, Puerto Rico. Between the 1493 discovery and 1508 the island was visited by the Spanish but never colonized until the later year by Ponce de León.

COLUMBUS, DIEGO, c1480-1526. Son of Christopher Columbus. He was named Governor of the Indies in 1508, and substituted Governor Ovando in that position in 1509. In this post he had serious disputes with the Crown and Ponce de León over his rights to his father's preogatives in the Indies. He opposed the naming of Ponce as Governor in Puerto Rico. In 1511 he won this case. In 1514 he unsuccessfully sought to found the town of Daguao in eastern Puerto Rico. The town was soon destroyed by Indians.

COMENDADOR MAYOR. Title held by persons in charge of administering a religious order or a military district. Nicolás Ovando held this title as the first Governor of the Indies. It was a title from the Order of Alcántara of which he was a knight. See also OVANDO, NICOLAS.

COMERIO. Municipio in the central, tobacco-producing region of the island. It was originally named Sabana del Palmar; its name was changed by a royal decree of 1894. Area: 28 square miles. Population: 18,819.

COMISIONADO RESIDENTE see RESIDENT COMMISSIONER

COMMONWEALTH OF PUERTO RICO. The official name of the government of Puerto Rico. It came into being with the ratification of the Commonwealth Constitution in July

1952, with the approval of both the U. S. Congress and the Legislature of Puerto Rico. The significance of Commonwealth status depends on ones' acceptance of the validity of the thesis that relations between Puerto Rico and the United States now rest upon a bi-lateral compact, rather than unilateral congressional action as under the Organic Acts of 1900 and 1917. Under Commonwealth status the islanders elect their own governor, legislature and local officials, and are generally self-governing in local affairs. Puerto Ricans, although U. S. citizens, do not have a vote for U. S. President or voting representation in Congress. The island is also subject to most federal laws of general application, such as compulsory military service, tariffs, coastwise shipping, customs, defense, foreign affairs and the mail service.

EL COMPONTE. A term used to describe a series of actions taken by Governor Palacios in 1887, to combat liberalism, principally within the Autonomist Party. These measures included torture, oppression, espionage and violent persecutions in order to obtain confessions.

CONCEPCION VASQUEZ, ANGEL DE LA, 1790-1841. Franciscan priest and respected professor who held chairs in both philosophy and chemistry. He was impeded from establishing physics and chemistry positions at the seminary, however, perhaps because of his fervent constitutional ideas which were in conflict with those of most of the church authorities.

CONSEJO DE INDIES. The supreme governing body set up in Spain in 1524 to administer the new colonies in America after the Discovery.

CONSTITUCION DE CADIZ, 1812. This document represented a large measure of representation for the overseas Spanish colonies. They would be represented in a newly established Cortes (parliament) and the absolutist monarchy would be terminated. It was redacted at the time of growing independence movements in the New World, and when Napoleon was taking over control of Spain. This constitution established deputies to be elected in the overseas colonies. Ramón Power was the first Puerto Rican to hold this post. By 1814 the king had declared the constitution null. It was then re-established from 1820-1823, eliminated once more, then restored again in 1836. However, in 1836, it was not applied to the Antilles. See also LEYES ESPECIALES, 1837.

CONSTITUCION PROVISORA DE LA REVOLUCION PUERTORRIQUEÑA. A provisional constitution designed to establish an independent government. It was signed January 10, 1868, in Santo Domingo by the four members of the "Revolutionary Committee": R. Betances, C. E. Lacroix, R. Mella and M. Ruiz Quiñones, secretary.

CONTINENTAL. A term used to identify persons from the continental United States. It is somewhat equivalent to the term "peninsular," used formerly to identify persons native to Spain.

CONUCO. Large tracts of unmeasured land, which included an Indian settlement (ranchería) led by a chieftain, nobility and the accompanying worker class. Ponce de León established the first of these on the lands of the leading chief Agüeybana. The conuco was also an agricultural unit and Ponce made profits from the sale of the right to use the conucos he established. He had to remit 20% of the profits to the king, while the Crown also retained ownership of the land. The Spaniards also used the word conuco to denote the straw huts used by the Indians living on these tracts.

COQUI. Tiny frog indigenous to the island and thought by many to be found only in Puerto Rico. It makes its characteristic "ko key" call at night.

CORAMBRE. Name given to uncured cowhides which were exported from Puerto Rico in the 16th century. The high tax on these resulted in the decline of their export by 1550.

EL CORAZON NEGRO. A secret society in Yauco municipio in the year 1887. This was a time of severe oppression of liberalism by Governor Palacios. See also EL COMPONTE.

CORCHADO Y JUARBE, MANUEL M., 1840-1884. A writer of many talents including poetry, drama and the essay. He co-founded in 1866, in Barcelona, the magazine Las Antillas, a political, scientific and literary publication. He sought to renew cultural Spanish life through his journalism. After returning to Puerto Rico in 1879, he dedicated his efforts to backing assimilation of the island with Spain.

CORDERO Y MOLINA, RAFAEL, 1790-1868. An outstanding, dedicated teacher. Cordero was the son of free Negroes. He opened a free school for Negroes and mulattoes, while working as a shoemaker to support his family.

CORDILLERA CENTRAL. The principal mountain range in Puerto Rico. It runs east from Mayagüez on the west coast, two-thirds of the length of the island. This large geographic region occupies 19 % of the total land area. Its peaks range generally from 2, 000 feet up to a maximum height of 4, 398 feet. It is the coffee-producing region of the country, with abundant orange and banana trees used to shade the coffee plants.

CORDOVA, PEDRO. A Dominican priest of the early 16th century. Along with Alonso Manso he was named Inquisitor of the Indies in 1519.

CORDOVA DIAZ, JORGE LUIS, 1907- . The Resident Commissioner to Washington, 1969-1972. He is also a lawyer, ex-justice of the Supreme Court, and long-time Statehood leader.

COROZAL. Municipio. Officially founded in 1795. Area: 42 square miles. Population: 24, 545.

CORPORACION DEL DESARROLLO ECONOMICO DEL CARIBE (CODECA). An innovative attempt by the Puerto Rican government to initiate economic cooperation within the Caribbean. Begun in 1965, as an outgrowth of the defunct Caribbean Organization, CODECA is a public corporation. Its plan was to stimulate economic cooperation through flexible voluntary agreements, with a minimum of ratification treaties. Members were drawn from islands of the eastern Caribbean, plus Puerto Rico, the Virgin Islands and the Dominican Republic. While CODECA was actively pushed under the Sánchez Administration (1965-1968), it was virtually disbanded when Governor Ferré and the PNP took over in 1969. Its revival is expected under the Popular Party Administration brought back to power in the 1972 election.

CORREGIDOR. The title of Capitán y Corregidor of San Juan was given to Vicente Yáñez Pinzón when he was granted the concession to found a colony in Puerto Rico in 1505. He never completed this task, however, merely stopping briefly at the island. In 1850 the title of corregidor was applied to the administrative heads of the ten principal towns in Puerto Rico, while the lesser towns retained the title of mayor. A corregidor is a magistrate who exercises royal jurisdiction in a given territory.

CORTES, HERNAN, 1485-1547. Famous conquistador of the Aztec Empire in Mexico. He reportedly used horses raised in Puerto Rico in carrying out this enterprise, and was sent aid from the island for the conquest.

CORTON Y DEL TORO, ANTONIO, 1854-1913. Poet, writer, critic and journalist. He became involved in island politics as a backer of a liberalized colonial regime, and in 1889 was elected deputy to the Spanish parliament.

CRAB ISLAND see under <u>Virgin Islands</u> portion of this Dictionary.

CRIOLLO [or Creole]. A person born in Puerto Rico, as opposed to the "peninsular" who was a native of Spain.

CRUZ MONCLOVA, LIDIO, 1899- . Outstanding Puerto Rican historian. Especially noted for his extensive history of the 19th century.

CUERDA. Unit of land measurement. Equivalent to 4,000 square meters, or slightly less than one acre.

CUERPO DE BOMBEROS. Fire department. The first in Puerto Rico was authorized by a law of 1841. It was established in 1846 under Governor Mirasol in San Juan. In Mayagüez the first company was formed in 1878.

CULEBRA. Tiny off-shore island municipality pertaining to Puerto Rico. It is located some 17 miles northeast of the island. Its cabecera, Dewey, contains most of the inhabitants. Culebra was not settled until the 19th century, mainly due to lack of rainfall and sparse vegetation. It has been much in the news in 1972 because of controversy over its use as a practice target for gunnery by the U. S. Navy, which has a large installation here and in the surrounding area. Area: 10 square miles. Population: 732.

CUMBERLAND, EARL OF see CLIFFORD, SIR GEORGE

- D -

DAGUAO. An early 16th-century town which was located at the present site of Naguabo municipio. It was originally founded by Captain Juan Henríquez, under orders from Diego Columbus. It was soon destroyed in 1514 by hostile Carib Indians. The name Daguao comes from the Boriquén Indian chieftain Daguao, or the Daguao River along whose banks it was founded.

DANZA. Musical piece accompanied by a special dance. It is composed of two parts, preceded by an introduction called the "paseo." The criollo danza was cultivated by leading musicians in past centuries and considered a symbol of Puerto Rican-ism.

DECIMA. A popular poetic form, usually sung by countryfolk and accompanied by music of the "triple" or "cuatro," guitar-like instruments.

DECLIEU, GABRIEL. French captain and 18th-century Governor of Martinique. He introduced the first coffee plants into the Antilles in 1720. Coffee became generally cultivated in Puerto Rico after 1768. See also COFFEE.

DEFIANCE. The English frigate commanded by Sir Francis Drake in his unsuccessful attack on San Juan in 1595. See also DRAKE, SIR FRANCIS.

DEGETAU GONZALES, FEDERICO, 1862-1914. An art lover, Degetau was a talented painter as well as orator and lawyer. In 1887 he founded a newspaper in Spain from which he attacked the despotic colonial government in Puerto Rico. He was elected to represent the island in the Spanish Cortes at the end of the 19th century. Under U. S. sovereignty of the island he became the first Resident Commissioner to Washington, in 1901.

DIARIO ECONOMICO. The island's first commercial newspaper, founded in 1814 by the Intendent, Alejandro Ramirez.

DIAZ, "PEPE." A late 18th-century folk hero, due to his heroic death in defense of the island during the 1797 attack by the English fleet. He became symbolic of the earliest criollos, or "Puerto Ricans."

DIEGO, JOSE DE, 1866-1918. One of the nation's leading politicians, poets, writers and orators. He established one newspaper and edited another. When the Autonomous Government of 1897 was established under Spain, he became the Assistant Secretary of Government. After the U. S. takeover he held high posts, including legislative leader from 1907-1918. He was also President of the Union Party. In 1904 he ardently spoke out for absolute sovereignty and became a staunch defender of national independence in his last years.

DIEZMOS. Taxes paid in the form of a percentage of the thing grown or produced. It consisted of remitting one-tenth, or one of each 10 things produced. It was established by the Bull of Alexander VI in 1501, and conceded to the Catholic Kings. Of this income a small portion was to go to the king, the rest for the construction and maintenance of the churches. It was abolished in 1810.

DIPUTACION PROVINCIAL DE PUERTO RICO. An elected governing body. It was first installed in Puerto Rico in August, 1813, upon the implementation of the Spanish Constitution of 1812. See also CONSTITUCION DE CADIZ, 1812.

DISTRITO. An administrative, political, judicial and electoral division. The island is divided into eight such districts. Constitutionally these constitute the basis for the election of the Senate. Each elects two senators to the island's legislature. Within the Senate districts are 40 Representative districts, each sending one representative to the House of Representatives. Every ten years both the Senate and House district lines are redrawn to reflect changes in the distribution of population.

DORADO. Municipio on the north coast. It officially attained the status of a town in 1842. The tourist boom of the 1960's had a large effect here due to the excellent beaches and construction of luxury hotels in the area. Area: 23 square miles. Population: 17, 388.

DRAKE, SIR FRANCIS, ca. 1543-1596. An English admiral who became the most famous seaman of Elizabethan times. His enemies considered him a pirate. He made the first circumnavigation of the world by an Englishman, 1577-1580. In 1595 he unsuccessfully attacked El Morro fortress at San Juan harbor, as the commander of a 27-ship expedition.

- E -

EIGHTEENTH CENTURY. Puerto Rico's economic, political and population development continued very slowly throughout this century. Even by the end of the century there were only 75, 000 whites. It was thus a poor, weak Spanish colony, which could be described as having implanted the Catholic religion, developed a fervent cult of the mother country Spain, and instituted a patriarchal family life. But commerce and agriculture were in ruin, with smuggling the national pastime. See also SMUGGLING.

E. L. A. see ESTADO LIBRE ASOCIADO

ELZABURU Y DE VIZCARRONDO, MANUEL, 1851-1892. Writer, poet, lawyer and journalist. He is especially known as the founder of the Ateneo Puertorriqueño in 1876. In 1878 he collaborated with José Gautier Benítez in founding the magazine, Revista Puertorriqueña de Literatura y Ciencias. His interest in the fine arts was interspersed with his legal practice so that frequently his law office became the site of literary meetings and informal chats. Elzaburu also became politically active, becoming one of the directors of the Partido Liberal Reformista.

ENGLISH ATTACK ON SAN JUAN, 1595 see DRAKE, SIR FRANCIS

ENGLISH CAPTURE OF SAN JUAN see CLIFFORD, SIR GEORGE

ENGLISH SIEGE OF 1797 see ABERCROMBY, SIR RALPH

ESCORIAZA Y CARDONA, JOSE EURIPIDES DE, 1828-1921. A criollo who became involved in Spanish politics, was implicated in a conspiracy plot in 1866, and forced to flee to France. When his fellow conspirators were later successful he returned to Spain to hold the posts of Governor of Almería, Valledolid and Barcelona. In 1868 he was elected to represent Puerto Rico in the Spanish parliament. He was an assimilationist, backing integration with Spain, but with equal rights and independence from absolutism.

ESCUDO. Generic name for certain coins of gold and silver. The name, meaning coat of arms, is derived from the imprinting of coats of arms on the reverse side of the coins. This class of coin was first mentioned in Spain in 1537. The Spanish monetary reforms of 1865 made the escudo the basic monetary unit in Puerto Rico as of July, 1865.

ESTADISTA. Person identified with the movement or parties seeking to annex Puerto Rico to the United States, as the 51st State.

ESTADO LIBRE ASOCIADO DE PUERTO RICO. The official name in Spanish of the Government of Puerto Rico. Literally, it means "Free, Associated State." However, the official English translation is Commonwealth of Puerto Rico (which see).

ESTRELLA, CAVETANO. Leader of the tiny uprising at Camuy in 1873 against the Spaniards. See also GRITO DE CAMUY.

LA ESTRELLADA see GRITO DE CAMUY

- F -

FAJARDO. Municipio on the east coast. Originally founded in 1760, it helped to prevent smuggling into the island from the neighboring off-shore islands. It serves as a departure point for commuter ships and planes to outlying Culebra and Vieques islands. Area: 31 square miles. Population: 23,032.

FEDERACION UNIVERSITARIA PRO INDEPENDENCIA (FUPI). A radical leftist organization of university students. Their primary goal is to assist the struggle for independence. The organization has chapters on all the major campuses of the island, and it resembles the Students for Democratic Society in the U. S. It has become very closely identified as a youth branch of the Movimiento Pro-Independencia, which has recently become the Socialist Party. See also PARTIDO SOCIALISTA PUERTORRIQUEÑO.

FERNANDEZ JUNCOS, MANUEL, 1846-1928. A native of Asturias, Spain he went to Puerto Rico at the age of 12, later to become one of the island's outstanding literary figures. As a writer and journalist he defended the island's culture and autonomy.

FERRE, LUIS A., 1904- . Governor of Puerto Rico, 1968-1972. As founder and president of the New Progressive Party his electoral victory ended the 28-year domination by the Popular Party. He is a strong advocate of Statehood. Under the Statehood Republican Party banner he ran for governor in 1956, 1960 and 1964 all unsuccessfully. He is also one of the island's wealthiest businessmen.

FERRER, JOSE, 1912- . World famous dramatic actor, singer, producer and director.

FIESTA DE SANTIAGO APOSTOL. Annual July festival held in the village of Loiza Aldea, in honor of their patron saint James the Apostol. The townfolk parade in bright masks in costumes of African origin. The custom began under the Spaniards more than 300 years ago. Traditionally the revelers split into four groups, dressing in the typical manner of each--gentlemen, devils, old folks and insane. The village is an anomaly in Puerto Rico in that it continues to be predominantly Negro.

FIESTAS PATRONALES. Annual festivals held in honor of the patron saint of the town. Each of the island's towns celebrates these festivities at some time during the year.

FIGUEROA, RODRIGO DE. A judge of the "residencia" in 1519. He wrote a lengthy and interesting report to the king outlining the reasons for moving the seat of government from the original settlement at Caparra to the harbor location on the islet to the north. In 1521 the move was made, and it is the present site of the capital of Puerto Rico and the city of San Juan.

FIGUEROA CARRERAS, LEOPOLDO, 1884-1969. Lawyer, doctor and politician. He became one of the top leaders of the Statehood Republican Party and was a member of the legislature for nearly 40 years.

FLORIDA. Municipio which has just attained independent municipio status. It was formally a barrio of Barceloneta. Its population and area are not reported in the 1970 census.

FORT SAN ANTONIO. One of the many fortresses making up the fortifications of the city of San Juan. A Catalonian military engineer, Ignacio Mascaró, directed its construction in the 16th century. It was located at the rear entrance to the islet, while El Morro fortress stood at the main entrance to the harbor. The fort is no longer in existence.

FORT SAN GERONIMO. A small fortification built by the Spaniards at the eastern end of the islet of San Juan. Built adjacent to Fort San Antonio, it was designed to assist in preventing enemy approaches to the capital from the rear. It has been restored by the Institute of Culture, while the nearby forts, San Antonio and El Escambrón have only remnants remaining.

LA FORTALEZA. Official residence and executive office of the Governor of Puerto Rico. The oldest Government House in America. In 1533 the Spaniards built their first "castle" in Puerto Rico, on the San Juan harbor. It was medieval in style and was built within the new walls around the city. This original structure, greatly altered and expanded is today's Fortaleza, known officially as El Palacio de Santa Catalina. Major remodeling and reconstruction took place in the 1640's and in 1846. It was twice briefly occupied during the Spanish period: in 1598 by the English under Clifford and in 1625 by the Dutch under General Hendrick.

F. U. P. I. see FEDERACION UNIVERSITARIA PRO INDEPENDENCIA

- G -

LA GACETA DE PUERTO RICO. The first newspaper in Puerto Rico, it was the official government gazette. The paper began publishing in 1806 in a building facing Columbus Square in San Juan.

GANGUIL. A small boat, using only one paddle. It was employed for rescue on the high seas in colonial times. The bow and the stern were similar so that the boat could be rowed either backward or forward.

GARCIA MENDEZ, MIGUEL A., 1902- . Politician, lawyer and wealthy businessman. In the 1930's he held prominent party and elective posts under the Partido Unión Republicano banner. Later, as maximum leader of the Partido Estadista Republicano in the 1950's and 1960's he led the campaign for Statehood. In the late 1960's he split with Luis A. Ferré and he and his party went into political obscurity after the 1968 election.

GARCIA TROCHE Y PONCE DE LEON, JUAN. Grandson of Juan Ponce de León, conquistador of Puerto Rico. García Troche is credited with being the first chronicler of the island. He inherited many privileges and positions through his family, such as Alcalde of the Casa Fuerte where the arms and munitions were stored. He was also the Official Treasurer, Accountant and Councilman of San Juan. See also MEMORIA DE MELGAREJO.

GAUTIER BENITEZ, JOSE, 1850-1880. Poet and journalist. Gautier is the most representative Puerto Rican romanticist of the 19th century.

GINGER. One of the many crops grown widely during Spanish colonial times which has since passed out of existence. In 1644 it was the leading crop produced, although just a few years later it began to decline in importance.

GOICO, PEDRO GERONIMO, 1808-1890. Physician, politician, professor and vigorous opponent of slavery. He became President of the Partido Liberal Reformista in 1870 and strongly defended the rights of criollos. Due to this stance he was considered an "enemy of Spain," so that when a 1866 military sedition incident occurred, although he was not involved, the authorities sought to expel him forever. But in 1868 he returned to Puerto Rico thanks to a change in the Spanish government. However, the Grito de Lares uprising that year caused his arrest again. He also served as President of the Sociedad Económica de Amigos del País.

GOLD. The lure of gold was one of the stimuli for Ponce de León's expedition of conquest and exploration in 1508. In the early 16th century the rivers were said to be rich with gold. The Indians were put to the task of mining gold, and it was first processed at Caparra in 1510. By 1536 the exploitation of mines had ended. These mines had rendered a total of some four million pesos worth of gold. After this, the colony failed to attract substantial population until the 19th century.

GONZALES CHAVEZ, JUAN, 1820-1865. Spanish born, he became the first person to introduce the art of bookbinding into Puerto Rico, and was among the first editors of books by Puerto Rican authors.

GONZALES DE LINARES, FRANCISCO. The first to occupy the separate post of civil governor, with the title Jefe Superior Político. Previously, military and civilian authority were held by the same person. Gonzales held this post for 18 months, 1822-1823, while Miguel de la Torre was military head. The posts were recombined after December, 1823.

GONZALEZ, JUAN. Friend and valuable ally of Juan Ponce de León, who accompanied him from Hispañola in 1508. González had learned to speak the Indian's language and knew much about their customs and society. He could even assume the appearance of an Indian, and thus succeeded in making friendly contacts for Ponce. He also put this to use on later espionage missions among the Indians.

GOVERNOR. The top executive official of Puerto Rico. At various times under the Spanish this official carried the title of Capitán General. Also, some Alcaldes Mayores served as the top executive. More than 140 persons served as governor under the Spanish from 1508-1898, including several acting governors. Seventy-five of these were military officers, as were all but three of the 46 governors serving from 1838-1898. After the United States assumed sovereignty the governors were named by the U. S. President, from 1898-1948. In 1948 the first Puerto Rican was popularly elected as governor, under the provisions of the Elective Governor Act, passed by Congress in 1946. See the following three entries.

GOVERNORS APPOINTED BY SPAIN. (These include Alcaldes Mayores and Ordinarios who sometimes headed the government when there was no official governor.)

Juan Ponce de León: August 1509 to October 1509.
Juan Cerón (Alcalde Mayor): October 1509 to March 1510.
Juan Ponce de León: March 1510 to 1511.
Juan Cerón 1511-1513.

(The above period was marked by bitter controversey over the rights to name the governor, between the King and Diego Columbus, inheritor of the Discoverer's rights. Further details of this are found under PONCE DE LEON, JUAN; and COLUMBUS, DIEGO.)

Rodrigo de Moscoso 1512-1513.
Cristóbal de Mendoza 1513-1515.
Juan Ponce de León 1515-1519.
Antonio de la Gama 1519-1521.
Pedro Moreno 1521-1523.
Alonso Manso (acting) 1523-1524.
Pedro Moreno 1524-1529.
Antonio de la Gama 1529-1530.
Francisco Manuel de Lando 1530-1536.
Vasco de Tiedra 1536-1537.
Alcaldes Ordinarios 1537-1544 (see also ALCALDES ORDINARIOS).
Gerónimo Lebrón 1544.
Iñigo López Cervantes de Loaisa 1545-1546.
Diego de Caraza 1546-1548.
Alcaldes Ordinarios 1548-1550.
Luis de Vallejo 1550-1555.
Esteves 1555.
Diego de Caraza 1555-1561.
Antonio de la Gama Vallejo 1561-1564.
Francisco Bahamonde de Lugo 1564-1568
Francisco de Solís 1568-1574.
Francisco de Obando y Mexia 1575-1579.
Gerónimo de Agüero Campuzano (acting) 1580.
Juan de Céspedes 1580-1581.
Juan Lopez Melgarejo 1581-1582.
Diego Menéndez de Valdés 1582-1593.
Pedro Suárez 1593-1597.

Antonio de Mosquero 1597-1598.
Alonso de Mercado 1599-1602.
Sancho Ochoa de Castro 1602-1608.
Gabriel de Roxas 1608-1614.
Felipe de Beaumont y Navarra 1614-1620.
Juan de Vargas 1620-1625.
Juan de Haro 1625-1630.
Enrique Enríquez de Sotomayor 1631-1635.
Iñigo de la Mota Sarmiento 1635-1641.
Agustín de Silva y Figueroa 1641.
Juan de Bolaños 1642-1643.
Fernando de la Riva Agüero 1643-1648.
Diego de Aguilera y Gamboa 1649-1655.
José Novoa y Moscoso 1655-1660.
Juan Pérez de Guzmán 1660-1664.
Gerónimo de Velasco 1664-1670.
Gaspar de Arteaga 1670-1674.
Diego Robladillo (acting) 1674.
Baltázar Figueroa (acting) 1674.
Alonso de Campos 1675-1678.
Juan de Robles Lorenzana 1678-1683.
Gaspar Martínez de Andino 1683-1685
Juan Francisco de Median 1685-1690.
Gaspar de Arredondo 1690-1695.
Juan Francisco de Medina (acting) 1695-1697.
Tomás Franco 1697-1698.
Antonio Robles (acting) 1698-1699.
Gabriel Gutiérrez de Rivas 1700-1703.
Diego Villarán (acting) 1703.
Francisco Sánchez (acting) 1703.
Pedro de Arroyo y Guerrero (acting) 1704-1705.
Juan Francisco Morla (acting) 1706.
Francisco Granados 1706-1708.
Juan de Ribera 1709-1715.
José Carreño (acting) 1716.
Alonso Bertodano 1716-1720.
Francisco Danio Granados 1720-1724.
José Antonio de Mendizábal 1724-1730.
Matías de Abadía 1731-1743.
Domingo Pérez de Mandares (acting) 1743-1744.
Juan José Colomo 1744-1750.
Agustín de Parejas 1750-1751.
Esteban Bravo de Rivero (acting) 1751-1753.
Felipe Ramírez de Estenós 1753-1757.
Esteban Bravo de Rivero (acting) 1757-1759.
Mateo de Guazo Calderón 1759-1760.
Esteban Bravo de Rivero (acting) 1760-1761.

Ambrosio de Benavides 1761-1766.
Marcos de Vergara 1766.
Jose Trentor (acting) 1766-1770.
Miguel de Muesas 1770-1776. Decreed racial integration in public schools.
José Dufresne 1776-1783.
Juan Dabán 1783-1789.
Francisco Torralbo (acting) 1789.
Miguel Antonio de Ustariz 1789-1792.
Francisco Torralbo (acting) 1792-1794.
Enrique Grimarest 1794-1795.
Ramón de Castro y Gutiérrez 1795-1804.
Toribio Montes 1804-1809.
Salvador Meléndez 1809-1820.
Juan Vascal y Pascual 1820.
Gonzalo de Aróstegui y Herrera 1820-1822.
José Navarro (acting) 1822.
Francisco Gonzáles Linares 1822-1823 (civil governor only).
Miguel de la Torre 1822-1837 (military governor only, 1822-1823).
Francisco de Moreda y Prieto 1837-1838.
Miguel López de Baños 1838-1841.
Santiago Méndez Vigo 1841-1844.
Rafael de Arístegui y Vélez 1844-1847.
Juan Prim 1847-1848.
Juan de la Perzuela y Cevallos 1848-1851.
Enrique de España Tiberner 1851-1852.
Fernando de Norzagaray 1852-1855.
Andrés García Gamba 1855.
José Lemery 1855-1857.
Fernando Cotoner 1857-1860.
Sabino Gamir (acting) 1860.
Rafael Echagüe 1860-1862.
Rafael Izquierdo (acting) 1862-1863.
Félix María de Messina 1863-1865.
José María Marchessi 1865-1867.
Julián Juan Pavía 1867-1868.
José Laureano Sanz 1868-1870.
Gabriel Baldrich 1870-1871.
Ramón Gómez Pulido 1871-1872.
Simón de la Torre 1872.
Joaquín Eurile (acting) 1872-1873.
Juan Martínez Plowes 1873.
Rafael Primo de Rivera 1873-1874.
José Laureano Sanz 1875.
Segundo de la Portilla 1875-1877.

Manuel de la Serna y Pinzón 1877-1878.
José Gamir (acting) 1878.
Eulogio Despujols y Dussay 1878-1881
Segundo de la Portilla 1881-1883.
Miguel de la Vega Inclán 1883-1884.
Carlos Suances Campo (acting) 1884.
Ramón Fajardo (acting) 1884.
Luis Dabán y Ramírez de Arellano 1884-1887.
Romualdo Palacios 1887.
Juan Contreras (acting) 1887-1888.
Pedro Ruiz Dana 1888-1890.
José Pascual Bonanza (acting) 1890.
José Lasso y Pérez 1890-1893.
Antonio Dabán y Ramírez de Arellano 1893-1895.
José Gamar 1895-1896.
Emilio March (acting) 1896.
Sabás Marín 1896-1898.
Ricardo Ortega (acting) 1898.
Andrés González Muñoz Jan. 11, 1898 (died 7 hours after taking office).
Ricardo Ortega 1898 (January and February).
Manuel Macías Casado 1898 (February to October).
Ricardo Ortega October 14-18, 1898.

GOVERNORS APPOINTED BY U. S. PRESIDENT.

John R. Brooke 1898. Named first governor during military government.
Guy V. Henry: December 1898 to May 1899.
George W. Davis: May 1899 to May 1900.
Charles Hubert Allen: May 1900 to September 1901.
William T. Hunt: September 1901 to July 1904.
Beeckman Winthrop: July 1904 to April 1907.
Regis H. Post: April 1907 to November 1909.
George R. Colton: November 1909 to November 1913.
Arthur Yager: November 1913 to May 1921.
José E. Benedicto: May 1921 (acting governor until Montgomery's arrival).
Emmet Montgomery Reilly: May 1921 to April 1923.
Horace M. Towner: April 1923 to October 1929.
Theodore Roosevelt: October 1929 to January 1932.
James R. Beverly: January 1932 to June 1933.
Robert H. Gore: July 1933 to January 1934.
Blanton Winship: February 1934 to August 1939.
William D. Leahy: September 1939 to December 1940.
Guy J. Swope: February 1941 to September 1941.
Rexford G. Tugwell: September 1941 to September 1946.
Jesús T. Piñero: September 1946 to January 1949 (First

and only Puerto Rican appointed governor by President.)

GOVERNORS POPULARLY ELECTED. (Terms begin in January.)
Luis Muñoz Marín 1949-1965.
Roberto Sánchez Vilella 1965-1969.
Luis A. Ferré 1969-1973.
Rafael Hernández Colón 1973- .

GRIFO. Person of generally white racial characteristics, but with some identifying Negroid racial feature.

GRITO DE CAMUY. A minor skirmish against Spanish authority in 1873. Led by Cayetano Estrella it was also referred to as "La Estrellada."

GRITO DE LARES. The proclamation of Puerto Rican independence from Spain, September 23, 1868. Some 400 men and women were involved, in the town of Lares, under the leadership of a Venezuelan, Manuel Rojas; a North American, Mathias Bruckman; and Puerto Ricans, Joaquín Parilla and Francisco Ramírez. The insurrection was very short-lived (one day) because of the general apathy of the population, lack of adequate military forces or training, and the prior knowledge of the plot discovered by the Spanish authorities. This latter factor forced the revolt to be carried out ahead of schedule, with the absence of its maximum leader, Ramón Betances who was outside the country. Island independence groups have annually commemorated the Grito's anniversary and it has become a semi-official holiday in recent years.

GUALBERTO PADILLA, JOSE. Known as "El Caribe," he was a leading 19th-century liberal spokesman. As such he was arrested and imprisoned as a suspect in the Lares Revolt of 1868. See also GRITO DE LARES.

GUANICA. Municipio on the south coast. The cabecera is located on a hill enclosed natural harbor, which was the site of the landing of U.S. forces in the War of 1898. It is also the site of the famous historical meeting between Ponce de León and the indigenous leader Agüeybana, in 1508. Although Guanica was one of the first settlements on the island, it attained municipio status only in 1914. Area: 37 square miles. Population: 14, 889.

GUANIN. The medallion-like adornments made from native gold which the Indian chieftains wore around their necks. This indicates that gold was given some special importance by the natives. These medals used by the Indians of Boriquén are thought to have come from outside the Antilles, via trade. Since the dead, even chieftains, were not given clearly marked burial places, these guanín have not been found and are only known through the accounts of early chroniclers.

GUAYAMA. Most populous municipio in the southeast region. It was founded in 1736 when it was a leading commercial center. Area: 65 square miles. Population: 36, 249.

GUAYANILLA. Municipio on the south coast. Its origins date back to the 18th century, but it was officially declared a municipio in 1833. Today it is the site of major petrochemical developments. Area: 42 square miles. Population: 18, 144.

GUAYNABO. Rapidly growing suburban municipio adjacent to San Juan. It was founded in 1723. Area: 27 square miles. Population: 67, 042.

GUERRA MONDRAGON, MIGUEL, 1880-1947. Lawyer, politico and literary figure. He is noted for being the first person publicly to put forth the idea of a Commonwealth--Estado Libre Asociado--in 1924.

GURABO. Municipio in the eastern region. Founded in 1815. Area: 28 square miles. Population: 18, 289.

GUARDIA NACIONAL. The National Guard was established in December, 1869 by Governor José Laureano Sanz. Unlike the popular militia it replaced, it was composed totally of Spaniards, thus serving to widen the gulf between Puerto Rican and Spanish interests.

- H -

HATILLO. Municipio; its cabecera is on the Atlantic coast. It was founded in 1823 as Hatillo del Corazón. Sugar cane and rum production abound here, making it one of the few places where agriculture is still the leading source of income. Area: 42 square miles. Population: 21, 913.

HATOS DEL REY. "Crown lands." The "hato" was a large tract of land, embracing some 10,000 square cuerdas. (The cuerda is equal to slightly less than one acre). In the 1770's there were some 234 hatos recorded.

HENDRICK, BOWDOIN [or Henrico, Boudoyno], ?-1626. A Dutch general whose forces successfully captured La Fortaleza in September 1625. The governor had fled to nearby El Morro fortress, however, and Hendrick was not able to force his surrender or capture the fort. He therefore set fire to La Fortaleza and other buildings before leaving the city. He reportedly died shortly thereafter, near Havana, as the result of a wound inflicted by the commander of El Morro during hand-to-hand fighting there. See also AMEZQUITA Y QUIJANO, JUAN.

HENNA, JULIO J., 1848-1924. A defender of independence under both Spanish and American rule. However, he originally aided the U.S. with information and sought to accompany U.S. troops in the War with Spain, thinking the U.S. would then grant independence. He was thus highly disillusioned by the Paris Peace Treaty of 1898.

HERACLIO RAMOS, ADOLFO, 1837-1891. Composer, pianist and music teacher. He was awarded several prizes for his compositions in the 1860's.

HERNANDEZ, RAFAEL, 1889-1965. An outstanding composer, many of whose more than 2,000 compositions are known widely in the Americas.

HERNANDEZ COLON, RAFAEL, 1936- . Governor-elect of Puerto Rico. Besides being a lawyer and author of various legal and political works, since 1965 he has been prominent in politics. In that year he became Secretary of Justice; in 1969 elected President of the Senate and of the Popular Democratic Party; and in 1972 was elected governor in a surprise sweeping victory. He thus becomes the youngest man, at 36, to occupy the post.

HERRERA, ANTONIO DE, 1549-1625. A Spanish chronicler of the Indies. In his four-volume work published in 1601, he dedicates a part to the discovery of Puerto Rico.

HORMIGUEROS. Small municipio adjacent to Mayagüez. The name means "ant hills," which reflects the nature of the hilly topography of the area. It attained municipio status in 1874, when it was separated from San Germán. In 1899, however, it became annexed to Mayagüez by order of General Guy Henry. It has since become a separate municipio again. Area: 11 square miles. Population: 10, 827. See also VIRGIN DE LA MONSERRATE.

HOSTOS, ADOLFO DE, 1887- . Historian and son of the famed hemispheric personality, María Eugenio de Hostos. Born in Santo Domingo, Hostos became the Official Historian of Puerto Rico in 1936. He has authored several historical studies of the island.

HOSTOS, EUGENIO MARIA DE, 1839-1903. Politician, writer, journalist and educator. Among the most illustrious Puerto Ricans in history, and truly a "citizen of the Americas." He fought for autonomy from Spain for the Antilles, abolition of slavery and an Antillian Confederation. In the late 19th century he became a more outspoken separatist. After the U. S. takeover in 1898, he tirelessly sought independence and a plebiscite for such status. He organized and directed various newspapers and magazines in several countries. He was an important educator in Chile and Santo Domingo, founding and directing various schools. He also authored some 50 books on wide-ranging topics.

HUMACAO. Municipio on the east coast. Declared a town in 1793. Area: 45 square miles. Population: 36, 023.

- I -

IGLESIAS PATIN, SANTIAGO, 1872-1939. Known as a "labor agitator" under Spanish rule, he was in jail at the time of U. S. occupation. In 1901 he went to the United States seeking support from Samuel Gompers and organized labor for his newly formed Labor Federation. By 1916 he had formed the Partido Socialista (Socialist Party) which sought statehood in addition to benefits for the workers. Under an electoral coalition with a party of quite opposite economic and social principles, Iglesias was elected Resident Commissioner to Washington in 1932. His death in 1939 and the rise of the

Popular Democratic Party in 1940, quickly sapped the strength of the Socialist Party and it disappeared shortly thereafter.

INDEPENDENTISTA. A person favoring the political status of a sovereign independent nation. A member of one of the pro-independence parties.

INDIAN REBELLION. A major rebellion of the indigenous Taino Indians occurred in 1511, under the leadership of Agüeybana II, and following the death of the chieftain Agüeybana, who had established good relations with Juan Ponce de León. The Indians had become more and more discontent with the enforced labor in the Spanish mines and hard working conditions. In the revolt, the governor's house was burned and many of the settlers were killed, including the aldalde mayor, Sotomayor. See also YAGÜECA.

INGENIO. Sugar mill. This term usually also implies the accompanying plantation and workers.

INSTITUTO DE CULTURA PUERTORRIQUEÑA. It was created in 1955 as an independent public corporation, its purpose being "to study and conserve the historical and cultural patrimony of Puerto Rico." It has been instrumental in restoring historical sites, promoting art workshops and artisan fairs, and publishing several works.

INSTITUTO DE LA LITERATURA PUERTORRIQUEÑA see PAGAN, BOLIVAR

INTENDENTE. The post of Intendent was created in 1784, but its duties were carried out by the Governor until 1811. Dealing with treasury, fiscal and economic matters, this post became an important one under its first occupant Alejandro Ramírez. When Ramírez accepted the Intendency of Cuba post in 1817, he was replaced by an interim appointment, José Ramírez de Arellano, who remained until May 1818. At that time Juan Ventura Morales was named Intendent. But he died suddenly in September 1819 and was never succeeded in the post. See also RAMIREZ, ALEJANDRO.

INTER AMERICAN UNIVERSITY [or Universidad Inter Americana]. Established in 1912 in San Germán as a Polytechnic Institute, by a Presbyterian missionary. It first offered college level courses in 1921. The school received accreditation in 1944 and in 1956 took the name Inter American University (IAU). Today the university consists of two main campuses in San Germán and San Juan, with several regional colleges. There is also a Law School and some graduate programs. Total enrollment has passed 10, 000.

ISABELA. Municipio on the north coast. It was founded in 1819 under the name San Antonio de la Tuna. Area: 56 square miles. Population: 30, 430.

- J -

JALDA. A steep hill or mountain. "Jalda Arriba" was the Popular Party's slogan for economic progress.

JAYUYA. Municipio in the central mountains, with the highest mountain peak, Cerro de Punto, 1, 338 meters. It became a municipio in 1911. In 1950 it was one of the key points of attack of the Nationalist Revolution, falling under the brief control of the revolutionaries before the arrival of the National Guard. Area: 39 square miles. Population: 13, 588.

J. E. E. see JUNTA ESTATAL DE ELECCIONES

JIBARO. The term used to designate the campesino, or peasant, who resides in the hilly, rustic setting. With modernization and urbanization since the 1940's, the countryside has lost vast numbers of peasants, while others have adopted urban culture. Presently the virtues of jíbaro culture have become identified with "puertorriqueñidad," so that even the pro-statehood Governor Ferré has described the ideal of "Jibaro Statehood."

JUANA DIAZ. Municipio in the south coastal region. It became an independent municipio in 1798. Area: 61 square miles. Population: 36, 270.

JUEGO [or Pelea] DE GALLOS. Cockfight. This sport was first established in April, 1770. Later it was abolished by the government, but again reestablished in 1782. It continues to be very popular, perhaps the most widely attended year-round spectator sport on the island. Each town has its cockfighting arena where weekly contests are held amidst lively betting.

JUNCOS. Small rural municipio in eastern Puerto Rico. Tobacco is a major economic activity. Area: 26 square miles. Population: 21, 814.

K: no entries

- L -

LABRA, RAFAEL MARIA, 1841-1918. Newspaperman, parliamentary lawyer, and specialist in Latin American problems. Cuban-born, Labra lived much of his life in Puerto Rico and Spain. He defended liberal reforms and the Antillian Colonial Law.

LAJAS. Municipio on the southwest coast. Formerly a barrio of San Germán, it became a municipio in 1883. The Lajas Valley has been an area of rich agricultural production, with sugar cane, pineapples and cattle raising especially important. Area: 60 square miles. Population: 16, 545.

LANDO, FRANCISCO MANUEL DE. Governor of Puerto Rico, 1530-1536. He took office at the time of rapid de-population and emigration due to poverty, and destruction caused by frequent hurricanes. To persuade the colonists to remain, Lando offered a moratorium on their debts and other prudent measures. Many consider him the most distinguished governor of the 16th century. He is noted for pointing out to the Crown the island's crucial strategic position in the West Indies.

LARES. Municipio established in 1827. It takes its name from a 16th-century colonizer Amador de Láriz who settled near here. Its location in the heart of the mountainous western side of the island puts it in the center of the coffee-producing region. It was the site of the 1868 independence revolt and an annual celebration commemorating the event is held here. Area: 62 square miles. Population: 25, 263. See also GRITO DE LARES.

LARRINAGA, TULIO, 1847-1917. Engineer, politician and orator. He became elected the second Resident Commissioner to Washington, 1905-1910.

LEDRU, ANDRES PIERRE. A French naturalist whose travels to Puerto Rico in 1797 are recorded in Viaje a la Isla de Puerto Rico. The Ledru expedition was typical of the 18th century, that period often called the "Era of Scientific Expeditions."

LEON AMERICANO (pseudonym) see DIEGO, JOSE DE

LEY DE 500 ACRES see AGRARIAN REFORM

LEY FORAKER see ORGANIC ACT OF 1900

LEY JONES see ORGANIC ACT OF 1917

LEY QUIÑONES-VARELA. A significant piece of legislation enacted by the Spanish Cortes in March, 1823. Its official title was "Instruction for the Political and Economic Government of the Overseas Provinces." Its authors were Puerto Rican deputy José M. Quiñones and Cuban delegate Félix Varela. Its substance was based on an amended version of the 1812 Spanish Constitution. Significantly, it represented an evolution of colonial policy from an assimilation to an autonomy orientation. While it specifically provided for the establishment of municipal, national and colonial governmental structures, its overriding impact was the incorporation of the principle that the overseas provinces were to be governed by laws applicable to their differing conditions. Just a week after the law's passage, Spain was invaded by the forces of the Quadruple Alliance, seeking to restore the Spanish absolutist regime. The law never went into effect as a result.

LEYES ESPECIALES, 1837. When the Constitution of Cádiz of 1812 was restored in Spain in 1836, both the governors of Cuba and Puerto Rico, Miguel Tacón and Miguel de la Torre, informed Spain that it was not wise to introduce these political reforms into the Antilles. Thus, the Spanish Cabinet named a 16-member committee of the Cortes to study this situation. The committee report of February 1837 recommended that the naturals of Cuba and Puerto Rico be excluded from a vote in the Cortes. In April 1837 a royal order was thus proclaimed providing that Special Laws (Leyes Especiales) be established for the Antilles. In Cuba the reaction against this law was particularly strong.

LA LIBRETA. The libreta system was established by Governor Juan de la Pezuela in June 1849. This law required that the local authorities maintain a register of all the day laborers in their district who were 16 years of age or older. Each worker in turn was to be given a "libreta," or notebook, in which his boss would note regularly his conduct in his job. Loss of the libreta carried a penalty of eight days' public work at one-half wages. Many land-owners balked at this system and suffered fines for not carrying out their part. The system was also strongly attacked by the liberal press and especially by José Pablo Morales. See also MORALES, JOSE PABLO.

LIGA DE PATRIOTAS. An organization founded just after the U. S. arrival in 1898. Among the chief purposes of the League was to lobby in Washington for the holding of a plebiscite to give Puerto Rico the right to decide its future political status. The League also had pedagogic, cultural and civic aims. Among its leaders were Hostos, Zeno Gandía and Henna. The history of the organization was a short one, as little agreement existed as to its objectives.

LLORENS TORRES, LUIS, 1876-1944. Poet, essayist, dramatist and politician. His modernistic poetry was even a precursor in time to that of Rubén Darío.

LOIZA. Municipio on the north coast, just east of San Juan. Settlement began here early in the 16th century. Its name is taken from an Indian princess, Luiza, who died in an Indian attack at the side of her Spanish lover. The municipio was founded in 1719. One of the principal rivers, Río Loiza, passes through the municipio. Area: 53 square miles. Population: 39,062. See also LOIZA ALDEA.

LOIZA ALDEA. A small coastal village located within the municipio of Loiza. It is a unique village on the island, due to its annual July festival and an extremely high percentage of Negro population. The July festival in honor of their patron saint is marked by parades involving distinctly African-type costumes, music and dancing.

See also FIESTA DE SANTIAGO APOSTAL.

LOTERIA DE PUERTO RICO. The lottery was initiated by Intendent Alejandro Ramírez in 1814, with the first drawing held September 1st. Today the lottery continues to be very popular and a large source of revenue for the government.

LUQUILLO. Municipio on the north coast. The cabecera was founded in 1797. Luquillo beach is one of the best and most well known in the Caribbean. Losing its municipio status for a time, it regained it in 1914. Area: 26 square miles. Population: 10, 390.

- M -

MACHETE. Knife-like tool of various lengths. It is used for cutting sugar cane, or for clearing brush and weeds. It has also traditionally been used as a weapon in rural areas.

MANATI. Municipio on the north coast, founded in 1738. Pineapples as well as sugar cane are the major crops. Area: 46 square miles. Population: 30, 559.

MANCHA DE PLATANO. Literally "stain of the plantain," figuratively it is a popular peasant expression for referring to a typical Puerto Rican, especially a peasant.

MANSO, ALONSO, ?-1539. As Bishop of Puerto Rico he was named the Inquisitor in January, 1519, by Inquisitor General Alonso Manrique, Cardinal of Tortosa. He thus became the first Inquisitor in the New World. Manso had gone to Puerto Rico in 1512. He got into various disputes with the residents over collection of taxes for the church, and also with the king because the encomienda granting him Indians was withdrawn.

LAS MARIAS. Rural municipio in mountainous west-central Puerto Rico. Area: 44 square miles. Population: 7, 841.

MARICAO. Municipio in the western mountain region. It was founded in 1874. Crops include coffee, bananas and citrus fruits, while the municipio as a whole lies within the Maricao National Forest Reserve. Area:

37 square miles. Population: 5, 991.

MARIN, RAMON, 1832-1902. Teacher, poet and dramatist. He founded several educational institutions, but throughout his teaching career he was harassed by Spanish authorities because of his stance in favor of Puerto Rican liberties. Leaving teaching he became a journalist, founding various newspapers between 1875 and 1890, where he again faced Spanish censorship.

MARQUES, RENE, 1919- . One of the island's leading contemporary writers. His works include novels, short stories, plays and essays.

MARTINEZ DE ANDINO, VICENTE, 1758-1837. A minor military official who gained fame and promotion due to his valiant leadership in defense of San Juan during the English attack under Abercromby in 1797. See also ABERCROMBY, SIR RALPH.

MARTINEZ NADAL, RAFAEL, 1877-1941. Politician, lawyer, and newspaperman. He was a staunch defender of federal statehood and the founder of the Partido Republicano Puro in 1924.

MATIENZO CINTRON, ROSENDO, 1855-1913. A leading political figure of his time. He backed Muñoz Rivera in forming a pact with the Spanish liberals in 1897 (see SAGASTA PACT). Under the first Organic Act of 1900, he was named to the Executive Council. Matienzo organized the first agricultural cooperative and started the idea of founding a movement of unity to demand from Congress the solution to the status problem. By this time, 1911-12, Matienzo had become dissillusioned with the idea of statehood and instead saw independence as necessary. He was also noted for combating monopolies and trusts. See also PARTIDO DE LA INDEPENDENCIA DE PUERTO RICO.

MATOS BERNIER, RAFAEL, 1881-1939. Liberal politician and newspaperman. He was director of La Democracia newspaper from 1912-13, and among the top leadership of the Union Party.

MAUNABO. Municipio along the southeast coast. It was declared a town in the late 18th century. Crops include sugar cane and fruit. Area: 21 square miles. Population: 10, 792.

MAYAGÜEZ. Municipio along the west coast. Although founded in 1760, much of the original cabecera was destroyed by fire in 1841. In 1877 it was declared a city by King Alfonso XII. It takes its name from the Yagüez River which empties into the sea here. Historically Mayagüez was the center of hand needlecraft industry, but this is now done by machines. Other industries include large tuna and fruit canneries. Area: 77 square miles. Population: 85, 857.

MAVI [or Mabi]. A type of small tree whose bitter bark is fermented and made into a popular drink of light alcoholic content.

MEMORIA DE MELGAREJO. The popular name for a 16th-century report, prepared for the Governor Juan Melgarejo by the cleric Ponce de León y García Troche, and Antonio de Santa Clara. This historically valuable descriptive report on the island's geography and society was prepared in response to a petition by King Philip II in 1582. The king had sent an extensive questionnaire throughout the Indies seeking similar information for all the possessions.

MEMORIA DE O'REYLLY [or O'Reilly]. An important historical report which aids the understanding of conditions in Puerto Rico in the 18th century. This documented study was put together by Field Marshal Alejandro O'Reylly in 1765. He had been commissioned by the king to carry out a general inspection of the island.

MERCADO, ALONSO DE. A 16th-century governor. He was sent to Puerto Rico in 1599 with some 3000 men to recapture the city of San Juan from the English forces under Clifford and thereupon to be governor. With the delay in travel, the English had already abandoned the city when Mercado arrived, due to difficulties with an uncooperative population and an outbreak of dysentery. Mercado and some 400 troops remained and he assumed the post of governor.

MILICIA. The popular militia. It gave valuable service in defense against various foreign invasion attempts, but was eliminated by a suspicious Governor Sanz in 1869. This was soon after two militia officers had been implicated in the Lares Revolt of 1868. Unlike the militia, the National Guard which replaced it was composed only of native Spaniards. See also GUARDIA NACIONAL.

MILITARY GOVERNMENT. Following the Treaty of Paris in which Puerto Rico became a possession of the United States, a brief period of military government was established. This lasted from October 1898 until April 1900. The military made substantial changes in the Spanish political tradition, abolishing the parliamentary system, reorganizing the judiciary, and separating church and state.

MIQUEAR. A verb from the student lexicon, meaning to "goof off," or waste time.

MOCA. Municipio at the foot of La Tuna Mountains, between Mayagüez and Aguadilla. It was founded in 1772. Agriculture is the chief economic activity, with coffee the leading crop. Area: 51 square miles. Population: 22,361.

MONA ISLAND. Tiny island mid-way between Puerto Rico and the Dominican Republic. It thus lies some 50 miles west of the municipio of Mayagüez, of which it is administratively a part. Lacking in water and good soil, the island has no permanent inhabitants. However, hunting is popular here, with game including wild goats, birds, pigs and large iguanas. Area: 12 square miles.

MONA PASSAGE. The 100-mile-wide ocean channel running north and south between Puerto Rico and the Dominican Republic. It is one of the heaviest used shipping routes, connecting the Atlantic and Caribbean.

MONEDA MACUQUINA. A type of silver coin, without a rimmed edge, which circulated in Puerto Rico in the first half of the 19th century. The Intendent Ramírez had recommended in 1813 that the governor permit its introduction from Venezuela. At that time there was a sizeable emigration from Venezuela to Puerto Rico. By 1847 the governor had requested permission from the king to withdraw the coins from circulation, holding them responsible for the disappearance from the colony of all better quality money. However, this money was credited with boosting commerce, since the then existing paper money was discredited and refused the world over. The redemption of the macuquina coins with a

12.5 % discount rate for the purchase of Spanish coins, caused a large deficit in the local treasury. Special taxes were then levied on several agricultural products to help offset the losses.

MONGE, JOSE MARIA, 1840-1891. Poet and journalist. He has been called the representative of the "beatus ille" theme in Puerto Rican romanticism.

MONTE DEL RODEO. The historical name for the present-day Miramar section of San Juan. Currently a fashionable residential area, it is a small highland immediately overlooking the islet on which the old city of San Juan is located.

MORALES, JOSE PABLO, 1828-1882. Educator, journalist and versatile writer. In the 1860's he began expressing his ideas of liberalism and social justice. He defended the rights of workers and strongly attacked the "libreta" system required by colonial law. This system required each laborer to carry a notebook in which their conduct record was recorded. See also LA LIBRETA.

MORALES, JUAN VENTURA, ?-1819. The second person to occupy the important post of Intendent (not counting interim appointments.) He died just four months after being named to the post. See also INTENDENTE.

MOREL CAMPOS, JUAN, 1857-1896. One of the most popular Puerto Rican musical composers, especially of "danzas."

MOROVIS. Municipio in central Puerto Rico, founded in 1818. Area: 39 square miles. Population: 19,059.

EL MORRO. Officially known as El Castillo de San Felipe, this massive fortification guards the entrance to San Juan harbor. It was one of the bastions of Spanish defenses in the Americas. While attacked frequently, it fell only once, briefly, into the hands of the enemy, until the final defeat of the Spaniards by U. S. forces in 1898. The fortress' construction was begun about 1540 and by the late 18th century it reached its present form. It is excellently preserved and today stands as a U. S. Historical Monument.

M. P. I. (Movimiento Pro Independencia) See PARTIDO

SOCIALISTA PUERTORRIQUEÑO

MUNICIPIO. The basic political and local level administrative unit. Puerto Rico has 78 municipios, varying in size from less than 7 square miles to more than 120 square miles, and in population from less than 1000 to more than 600, 000 inhabitants. Each consists of a cabecera, an administrative urban center of the same name, and one or more rural barrios. In the highly centralized government the municipios are constitutionally creatures of the legislature, and they have only minor political influence. Each elects a mayor and assembly, with the number of assemblymen varying from 12 to 16, except in San Juan (17) and Culebra (5).

MUÑOZ MARIN, LUIS, 1898- . Journalist, writer and poet, but especially noted as a political leader and statesman. He has been the island's outstanding figure since 1940, gaining hemisphere-wide fame for his leadership in the transformation of Puerto Rico. As the son of an important 19th-century figure, Luis Muñoz Rivera, he was exposed to both journalism and politics. He founded the Popular Democratic Party in 1938. As leader of this party he carried out broad social and economic changes, in addition to becoming the first popularly elected governor, in 1948. Muñoz was re-elected by landslide victories until 1964, when he decided to step down from the post. See also PARTIDO POPULAR DEMOCRATICO.

MUÑOZ RIVERA, LUIS, 1859-1916. Poet, journalist, and political leader. He founded various newspapers, including La Democracia, El Liberal and El Diario de Puerto Rico. He was a particularly skillful orator and pragmatic politician. He was instrumental in obtaining a pact with the Spanish liberal leader Sagasta which led to the granting of an Autonomous Charter to Puerto Rico in 1897. Muñoz occupied high posts both before and after the U. S. presence, including that of Resident Commissioner to Washington where he struggled to obtain a more self-governing status. He organized both the Federal Party and its successor, the Union Party. Always the realist, he sought obtainable measures of autonomy and self-government, but his private correspondence indicates that his deepest long-term goal was that of independence.

- N -

NAGUABO. Municipio on the southeast coast. Originally its cabecera was built near the Caribbean coast, in 1794, but was moved inland in 1827. Area: 52 square miles. Population: 17, 996.

NARANJITO. Municipio founded in 1824, when residents of Bayamón and Toa Alta decided to form a new town. They were given a farm at the present site of the municipio. It officially attained municipio status in 1902. Area: 28 square miles. Population: 19, 913.

NATIONAL ANTHEM. The official hymn of the Commonwealth is called "La Borinqueña." The exact date of its composition is unknown, but it dates at least from the late 19th century. The music was composed by Félix Astol and the words were added by Lola Rodríquez de Tío. The melody was originally a danza, a serene harmonious type of music.

NATIONALIST REVOLUTION OF 1950. The first and only armed revolution against the United States in Puerto Rico. It was initiated by militants of the Nationalist Party on October 30, 1950. Small bands of nationalists attacked various police stations as well as the governor's residence at La Fortaleza. The only success, however, was the taking of the town of Jayuya for a short time, and the burning of federal buildings there. On the 31st of October, 1950, two nationalists attacked Blair House in Washington, where President Truman was in residence, and others began a shooting spree within the U. S. House of Representatives. These attacks resulted in the death of a guard and some of the attackers, while the rest were arrested. As a result of the "revolution" some 164 nationalists were convicted of various crimes. On November 23, 1972 Governor Ferré pardoned the last four imprisoned in Puerto Rico, while the five involved in the Washington shootings remain in federal prison in the U. S.

NEWSPAPERS. The earliest newspaper was the official government gazette, La Gaceta, begun in 1806. Today there are four daily papers, three in Spanish and one in English. El Mundo, El Imparcial and San Juan Star are all published in San Juan, while El Día, owned by the Ferré family, is from Ponce. The major political parties and groups also publish periodic newspaper-type publications. That of widest circulation is probably the weekly Claridad, published by the radical, independence-minded, Socialist Party.

NOCHE DEL JUA See Addendum p. 88.

NOVISIMA RECOPILACION. The recapitulation of Spanish laws made after Napoleon was defeated and driven from Spain.

NOVOA Y MOSCOSO, JOSE DE. Governor from 1655-1661. Novoa came to the post after a long and successful military career, beginning in a 1624 campaign in Naples.

NUEVA VILLA DE SALAMANCA see SAN GERMAN

- O -

O'DALY, DEMETRIO, 1780-1837. Born in San Juan, he pursued a military career and gained fame and promotion to the rank of general. He was also a notable political liberal and defender of the 1812 Constitution. He influenced King Ferdinand VII in restoring this constitution in 1820. In that same year Puerto Rico elected O'Daly as its representative to the Cortes. In the Cortes of 1820-21, he sought to punish violations of the constitution and declare the monarch incapacitated. He was then forced to flee to Puerto Rico, Europe, America and finally St. Thomas for some ten years.

OLLER, FRANCISCO, 1833-1917. Along with Campeche, Oller is the most famous painter of the 18th and 19th centuries. Emotion, nature and Catholic religious influences are seen in his work.

O'REYLLY, ALEJANDRO see LA MEMORIA DE O'REYLLY

ORGANIC ACT OF 1900. Known as the Foraker Law, this act of the U. S. Congress of April 12, 1900, established the provisions of the first civil government under U. S. sovereignty. The act followed two years of military rule after the Spanish-American War. Its provisions were disappointing to many Puerto Rican leaders, since under the Spaniards a more autonomous Charter had been authorized in 1897. The Foraker Law allowed popular election only of the lower house of the legislature, the mayors and other lesser municipal officials, plus a Resident Commissioner to sit in Congress without a vote. All other offices were left to presidential appointment, while the Congress reserved the right to annul insular legislative acts. Economically, this law put Puerto Rico within the U. S. tariff and fiscal system. While the act was termed "provisional" by Congress, it was in effect for 17 years.

ORGANIC ACT OF 1917. The Second Organic Act, or Jones Law, became effective in March, 1917. Extending somewhat local autonomy, an upper legislative chamber, the Senate, was created and made popularly elective. Other presidential and congressional perogatives continued in effect. Another innovation of this law was the extension of U. S. citizenship to Puerto Ricans, despite the objections by leaders such as de Diego that this would close the possibility to future independence. Citizenship brought with it the obligation of U. S. military service but not federal taxation.

OROCOVIS. Municipio. It was known as Barros at the time of its founding in 1825. The name Orocovis is derived from a pre-Columbian Indian chief named Orocobis who resided in the area. The town was largely destroyed by fire in 1875. Area: 63 square miles. Population: 20, 201.

OSUNA, JUAN JOSE, 1884-1930. An outstanding educator.

OVANDO, NICOLAS DE, c1451-1511. Spanish military leader and first Royal Governor of the Indies, 1501-1509. Ovando arrived at his post in Santo Domingo in 1502, with broad powers of jurisdiction and a large fleet. After pacifying the island of Hispañola he established a stable Spanish community that became the model for all later Spanish settlements. He authorized Ponce de León to conquer and settle Boriquén (Puerto Rico).

OVIEDO Y VALDES, GONZALO FERNANDEZ DE, 1478-1557. Spanish politician and historian. One of the best known historians of the colonization and conquest of the Indies. Coming to America for the first time in 1513 he made 11 voyages to the New World. He was designated Chronicler of the Indies. In 1535 he published the first part of a monumental 19-part work, Historia General y Natural de las Indias. Part 16 treats Puerto Rico.

- P -

P. A. C. see PARTIDO ACCION CRISTIANO

PADIAL Y VIZCARRONDO, LUIS, 1832-1879. A criollo, he was named an official in the Spanish army in Spain. He was an abolitionist and autonomist and became the first deputy to the Cortes to seek autonomous government for the Antilles.

PAGAN, BOLIVAR, 1897-1961. Lawyer, journalist, writer and politician. A staunch defender of statehood for the island, he was President of the Socialist Party and Resident Commissioner to Washington. He founded the Institute of Puerto Rican Literature and was its president, 1936-1940.

EL PALACIO DE SANTA CATALINA see LA FORTALEZA

PALES MATOS, LUIS, 1898-1959. A Negro poet especially devoted to Negro themes. He presents a bitter interpretation of Negro life in the Antilles.

PALMER, SANTIAGO R., 1844-1908. Journalist and politician. He helped found the Partido Liberal Reformista in Mayagüez in 1869. His career in journalism included the forming of various newspapers and attacks on the conservative Spanish regime. Palmer was named Mayor of Mayagüez when the American forces took possession in 1898. He is also known for his fervor in organizing the Masonic Lodge.

PAOLI, ANTONIO, 1872-1946. An international opera star. At one time he was called the "Tenor of Kings and King of Tenors."

PARILLA, JOAQUIN, ?-1868. One of the leading rebels in the Lares revolt of September 1868. After refusing to surrender, he was killed by Spanish forces on October 18. By the end of October the last rebel had been captured or shot. See also GRITO DE LARES.

PARTIDO. Geographical, administrative division used by Spain. In the 16th century, there were two large partidos: the Partido de Puerto Rico included the land east of the Camuy River on the north, to the Jacaguas River on the south; the Partido de San Germán included the rest of the island to the west of these boundaries. In a royal cédula of June, 1831, the creation of seven partidos was established, each headed by an alcalde mayor, and each having jurisdiction over several towns. At its implementation in 1832, some 58 towns were officially recognized and divided among these seven partidos. See also ALCALDE MAYOR.

PARTIDO ACCION CRISTIANO. Political party formed in 1960 by the impetus of two U. S. -born Catholic bishops. Vaguely resembling various western Christian Democratic parties, the PAC's real emphasis was on attacking Luis Muñoz Marín and the Popular Democratic Party policies toward birth control and education. After receiving limited support in 1960 and 1964 the party disappeared.

PARTIDO AUTENTICO SOBERANISTA. A tiny political party supporting independence. It was formed by Jorge L. Landing as a dissident group within the Independence Party, following the 1968 election. Since it received only a fraction of 1 % of the vote in 1972 it will no doubt cease to exist.

PARTIDO AUTONOMISTA. This political party was established at an assembly in Ponce, March 10, 1887. Its founder and first president was Román Baldorioty de Castro. Political events in Spain and on the island had left the existing Liberal Party factionalized and disorganized, when Baldorioty united them behind the idea of self-rule, under the banner of this new party. The platform and form of government it backed was known as the Plan de Ponce. Opposition harassment and internal division over tactic and ideology plagued the party. After Baldorioty's death in 1889 it could no longer be held together. See also PLAN DE PONCE.

PARTIDO COMUNISTA PUERTORRIQUEÑO. The Communist Party was first organized in 1933. It never gained more than a handful of supporters and is now (1972) totally defunct electorally and, for all practical purposes, exercises no political influence.

PARTIDO ESTADISTA REPUBLICANO. A now defunct political party since its leadership was nearly totally absorbed by the New Progressive Party in 1968. It was a long-time conservative, pro-Statehood force under its maximum leader Miguel Angel García Méndez. From 1917-1932 it was known as the Partido Republicano; from 1932-1948, Unión Republicano; in 1948 it became the Partido Estadista Republicano.

PARTIDO FEDERAL AMERICANO. Political party founded in October, 1899, under the leadership of Luis Muñoz Rivera. It was born out of the Partido Liberal, which had been dissolved with the change of sovereignty from Spain to the United States. The party supported the territorial status of the island as transitorial to federal statehood.

PARTIDO DE LA INDEPENDENCIA DE PUERTO RICO. The first organized political party backing independence from the United States. It was founded in 1912. Among its chief organizers was Rosendo Matienzo Cintrón, a disillusioned statehooder. Others of its founders were Dr. Pedro Franceschi, Manuel Zeno Gandía, Benítez Castano and Gandía Córdova.

PARTIDO INDEPENDENTISTA PUERTORRIQUEÑO. Political party founded in 1946 by uncompromising independentistas within Muñoz Marín's Popular Democratic Party. Many, if not most, of the original leaders of the Popular Party were independentistas when the party organized in 1938. But since Muñoz de-emphasized the status issue it attracted followers from diverse camps. By 1946 the more intransigent independentistas split with the Populares. The PIP's greatest electoral total came in 1952, when it obtained 19% of the vote. Since then it has declined and receives less than 5%. Internal dissention has always hampered the party, much of it over the proper stance toward the election process and the proper strategy for obtaining independence. The most recent prominent leader is Rubén Berrios, a young, fiery intellectual, who has led the party's recent commitment to socialism.

PARTIDO LIBERAL Political party founded about 1870, during Spanish rule. It became divided by the issue of the proper relation toward Spain and the Spanish political parties, in the late 1890's. From 1897 until 1899 it was known as the Partido Liberal Fusionista, since it was "fused" into the Spanish Liberal Party. It was dissolved in 1899 after the U. S. takeover of the island, converting into the Partido Federal Americano. See also SAGASTA PACT.

PARTIDO LIBERAL FUSIONISTA see PARTIDO LIBERAL

PARTIDO LIBERAL PUERTORRIQUEÑO. Political party founded in December 1931 as an outgrowth of the Union Party. The Union Party had become divided over a platform plank declaring itself in favor of independence for the island. This new Liberal Party went on to poll more votes than any single party in the elections of 1932 and 1936, but was defeated due to electoral coalitions formed by two opposing parties. Luis Muñoz Marín was one of the young, top leaders of the Liberal Party, when he became embroiled in a leadership struggle which led to his ouster and the formation of the Popular Democratic Party in 1938. Muñoz in fact took most of the party's leadership and electoral following with him and as a result, the Liberal Party soon disappeared.

PARTIDO NACIONALISTA. Political party founded in 1922. It created little attention until the 1930's when its leadership turned to militancy and violent acts in an effort to achieve its goal of independence. During this militant period its maximum leader was Pedro Albizú Campos, a popular, charismatic figure. During the 1950's the Nationalists attempted to assassinate President Harry Truman and Governor Muñoz Marín, as well as initiate an armed revolt throughout the island. See also NATIONALIST REVOLUTION OF 1950.

PARTIDO NUEVO PROGRESISTA. Political party founded in 1968 by Luis A. Ferré and dissenchanted followers of the Statehood Republican Party. It soared to instant success by winning the 1968 election, thus ending three decades of near one-party rule by the Popular Party. While the party platform calls for statehood, both in 1968 and 1972 it appealed to voters from all status preferences. Surprisingly it was soundly defeated in 1972 by the Popular Party.

PARTIDO DEL PUEBLO. Political party founded in 1964 which had gone unnoticed until 1968, when it gained glaring notoriety after it was totally "transferred" to Governor Roberto Sánchez Vilella. Sánchez, a Popular Party member, had split with his party and the People's Party thus provided a vehicle for his re-election attempt.

It won 10% of the vote in 1968, contributing greatly to the Popular Party's narrow loss. Its followers returned to the Popular Party in the 1972 election, leaving the People's Party with little support.

PARTIDO POPULAR DEMOCRATICO. The political party which dominated island politics from 1940-1968. It was founded in 1938 by Luis Muñoz Marín. The PPD became in effect the first modern political party, mobilizing the masses and pledged to modernization. It converted the political system into a nearly one-party system, since it won nearly every elective office during three decades. The party was built around its reform program of the 1940's and an extremely popular charismatic leader. This personalism led to dissention in the ranks after Muñoz decided to transfer leadership in 1964. A divided party lost the 1968 election. Its recovery and reorganization under Rafael Hernández Colón was obvious after winning the 1972 election with surprising ease.

PARTIDO REPUBLICANO PUERTORRIQUEÑO see PARTIDO ESTADISTA REPUBLICANO

PARTIDO SOCIALISTA. A defunct political party which competed in elections from 1917-1952. It was a labor party founded by Santiago Iglesias Patín in 1916. It advocated statehood and economic and social reforms. Highly personalistic, however, the party went into rapid decline with the death of its founder in 1939, and the rise of the reform-minded Popular Party in 1940.

PARTIDO SOCIALISTA PUERTORRIQUEÑO. Political party formed as the result of a November 28, 1971, assembly of the Movimiento Pro Independencia (MPI). Since 1961 the MPI, a radical off-shoot of the Independence Party, had preached boycotting of the whole electoral process. Not opposed to using violence, it proclaimed a Marxist-Leninist ideology. In 1971, the MPI sought to form an electoral front with the Independence Party, thus it made the move to convert itself into a political party. The coalition was not accepted, however, so the Socialist Party did not participate in the 1972 election.

PARTIDO UNION PUERTORRIQUEÑO. Another of the tiny independence parties that appeared as split-offs from the Partido Independentista Puertorriqueño after 1968.

Its leader is Antonio González. Since it received a tiny vote in 1972 it is not a viable political or electoral group.

PARTIDO UNION REPUBLICANO see PARTIDO ESTADISTA REPUBLICANO

P. A. S. see PARTIDO AUTENTICO SOBERANISTA

PATILLAS. Municipio on the south coast; founded in 1811 officially, but settlement began here in the 17th century. The establishment of sugar mills prompted the town's founding. Area: 48 square miles. Population: 17, 828.

P. C. P. see PARTIDO COMUNISTA PUERTORRIQUEÑO

PEDREIRA, ANTONIO S., 1899-1939. Poet, professor and literary figure. His many works illustrate a dedication to the study of Puerto Rican personality and culture.

PEÑUELAS. Municipio founded in 1793, adjacent to Ponce. Today it is the site of giant petrochemical and refinery complexes. Area: 44 square miles. Population: 15, 973.

PEPINO see SAN SEBASTIAN

P. E. R. see PARTIDO ESTADISTA REPUBLICANO

PESETA. Spanish monetary unit, which in Spain currently has the value of about 1. 5 cents (U. S.). In Puerto Rico the term peseta is used to denote the American 25-cent piece.

PESO. Spanish unit of money. This word is now used interchangeably with the English word dollar, meaning one dollar in U. S. currency.

PICA. Popular type of roulette; installed in booths around the public plaza as part of the traditional annual celebration of the patron saint festival of each town. See also FIESTAS PATRONALES.

LAS PIEDRAS. Municipio in eastern Puerto Rico. This high region is productive of tobacco and fresh fruits. It became a municipio in 1801. Area: 33 square miles. Population: 18, 112.

PIÑERO, JESUS T. First Puerto Rican to occupy the post of governor. The last American governor, Rexford G. Tugwell, had recommended to President Truman that a Puerto Rican be appointed to the post when Tugwell retired in 1946. Piñero, who at the time held the position of Resident Commissioner to Washington, occupied the governor's post from September 1946 until Muñoz Marín's inauguration as the first elected governor in January 1949.

P. I. P. see PARTIDO INDEPENDENTISTA PUERTORRIQUEÑO

PIRAGUA. Large canoes used by the Indians. In modern times, a popular refreshment made from shaved ice with fruit-flavored syrup poured over it has taken the name "piragua." Originally this icy treat was made in the shape of a canoe.

PLAN DE PONCE. The Ponce Plan was a political platform put together under the leadership of Román Baldorioty de Castro, at the founding of the Autonomist Party in Ponce in 1887. This document outlined the autonomous, as opposed to independent, government drawn up by the party assembly. It was signed by Luis Muñoz Rivera and José Celso Barbosa, as well as Baldorioty.

PLEBISCITE ON POLITICAL STATUS. On July 23, 1967, the first formal plebiscite on the island's political status was held. Prior to 1967, the holding of such a popular plebiscite had been proposed at least a dozen times, beginning in 1898. Alternatives to choose from included "culminated" Commonwealth (E. L. A. --which see), Statehood, and Independence. Commonwealth received 60.5% of the vote, Statehood 38.9%, and Independence 0.6%. The results were inconclusive in many respects, however. Only 66% of the eligible voters participated, both the Statehood and Independence Parties boycotted the plebiscite, and the U. S. Congress was in no way bound to honor the results.

P. N. see PARTIDO NACIONALISTA

P. N. P. see PARTIDO NUEVO PROGRESISTA

POLITICAL PARTIES. Parties in Puerto Rico can generally be described as highly centralized, lacking in ideological consistency, and having a personalistic leadership and strict discipline of members. While one party, the P. P. D., dominated politics from 1940 to 1968, today a two-party system may be emerging. Two types of parties are officially recognized by the electoral law, and may appear on the ballot. "Principal" parties are those whose candidate for governor in the last election received at least 5% of the total vote cast for all parties for all candidates for governor. Parties by "petition" are those who register petitions with the Election Board containing signatures totaling at least 5% of the total vote cast for governor in the most recent election. Six parties were on the ballot in the 1972 election; three principal parties and three by petition. Only two parties, the P. N. P. and P. P. D., obtained significant vote totals.

PONCE. Municipio on the south coast. The city of Ponce, its cabecera, is the second largest urban and commercial center of the island. Founded in the late 17th century, Ponce became a city officially in 1877. Its rich cultural heritage today is highlighted by an art museum donated by Governor Ferré. Several university campuses are here, there is an ocean port facility, and sugar cane, rum and cement are leading economic enterprises. Area: 116 square miles. Population: 158, 981.

PONCE DE LEON, JUAN, 1460-1521. Spanish conquistador and explorer. He came to America with Columbus on the second voyage in 1493. In 1508 he began the colonization of Puerto Rico, founding the first settlement at Caparra. After governing the island a few months by authorization of the Governor General of the Indies, Nicolás Ovando, Ponce ceded his position to the representative of Diego Columbus, (Ovando's replacement). But soon thereafter Ponce received the title of Governor from the king, dated August 1509. He then returned to Caparra and arrested Columbus' appointment, Juan Cerón, sending him to Spain as prisoner. In an ensuing legal battle, Columbus won the right to name the governor so Ponce resigned in 1511. He then left on a voyage of discovery and exploration, discovering Florida.

PONCE DE LEON, LUIS. Son of the conquistador Ponce de León. As such he inherited the titles and positions of his father. In 1524 he was granted the title of Alcalde of Puerto Rico (the capital city), and also Adelantado of Florida.

PONCE MASSACRE. This was a deadly confrontation between police and demonstrators from the Nationalist Party, in the city of Ponce, March 1937. Police action is generally blamed for the unprovoked attack and death of several unarmed persons. However, this was a period of high tension due to much violence by the Nationalists.

PORTA COELI. A historic church in San Germán. Among the oldest in the New World, it was built in the early 17th century. It has been restored by the Institute of Puerto Rican Culture, and converted into a museum of religious art.

POWER GIRALT, RAMON, 1775-1813. An outstanding politician and naval officer. While in the service of the Spanish Navy, Power contributed to the recovery of Spanish territory in the Caribbean. He was instrumental in directing the decisive victory over the French, which drove them out of Santo Domingo, recapturing the Spanish half of the island of Hispañola. In 1810 he was selected as Puerto Rico's first deputy to the Cortes in Spain, where his eloquence and popularity gained him the post of vice president, highest post held by a Puerto Rican in Spain. In the work of the Cortes he was instrumental in the passage of a law in 1811 which separated the office of Intendent from that of the Governor's office. Through Power's insistence Alejandro Ramírez was named to that post, and the latter aided immensely the commercial and economic development of the island.

P. P. see PARTIDO DEL PUEBLO

P. P. D. see PARTIDO POPULAR DEMOCRATICO

PRIMICIAS. Taxes collected from island residents by virtue of a royal order of 1511, which was not abolished until 1848. Like the diezmos, it was not a tax to be paid in money or gold, but rather as a percentage of the thing produced. For example, the tax (primicia) due for every six "fanegas" of produce was one-half a fanega (a fanega equals about 1. 6 bushels). See also DIEZMOS.

PROYECTO DE INSTRUCCION para el Gobierno Económico y

Político de las Provincias de Ultramar see LEY QUIÑONES-VARELA

P. S. P. see PARTIDO SOCIALISTA PUERTORRIQUEÑO

PUBLIC LIGHTING SYSTEM. This was established in San Juan in January 1820. Lanterns which burned olive oil were still in use at that time.

PUERTO DE MOSQUITOS. The port of Guanica. Historically it was often referred to as the port of mosquitos due to the plague of mosquitos found there by the Spaniards.

PUERTO RICO see COMMONWEALTH OF PUERTO RICO

P. U. P. see PARTIDO UNION PUERTORRIQUEÑO

- Q -

QUEBRADILLAS. Municipio on the north coast, founded in 1823. Area: 23 square miles. Population: 15, 582.

QUIÑONES, FRANCISCO MARIANO, 1830-1908. Spending his early years in Germany, Quiñones returned to San Germán, founding the newspaper El Espejo, from which he expounded his political ideal of autonomy. After Spain granted the Autonomous Charter of 1897, Quiñones presided over the Cabinet, in charge of the insular government. He later served as the representative from San Germán to the first legislature under American rule. Quiñones was a strong advocate of abolition of slavery in the 1860's.

QUIÑONES, JOSE MARIA, 1782-? Lawyer and deputy to the Spanish Cortes. He was elected to the 1813-1814 term, but never served in the Cortes since the Constitution of 1812 was nullified by King Ferdinand VII.

- R -

RAILROADS. In 1865 the Marqués de la Serna proposed the development of a railroad, but the proposal never was carried out. In 1878 the construction of a railroad around the island was authorized. By a royal decree of 1888, a 99-year concession for building such a railroad around the coast was granted to Ivo Bosch y Puig. After six years, in 1894, only some 200 of the 546 kilometers granted in the concession had been constructed. In 1902 the American Railroad Company was organized. It completed its first line in 1908, expanding widely by 1920. Railroads have since gone out of use on the island of Puerto Rico, with not a single line in operation.

RAMIREZ, ALEJANDRO, 1774-1821. Spanish liberal statesman and treasury expert. At the impetus of Ramón Power, he was named the first Intendent for Puerto Rico in 1812. In this position he did much to improve the economy of the island. He founded a society for advancing agriculture and industry, stimulated education and in 1814 founded the first commercial newspaper, Diario Económico. He also founded the lottery. He ran into conflicts with the Governor, Salvador Meléndez, over the loss of these economic powers from his office. In 1817 Ramírez left the post to become Intendent in Cuba. See also INTENDENTE.

RAMIREZ, ALONSO. A 16th-century adventurer whose fantastic voyage around the world is recorded in a 1690 work by the noted poet, Carlos de Sigüenza y Góngora. This same work has been termed by some scholars as the first completely novel-type publication to appear from Hispanoamérica.

RAMIREZ MEDINA, FRANCISCO. President of the Revolutionary Government established in Lares, September 23, 1868. Only three days later this independence insurrection was routed; Ramírez was captured on October 18. See also GRITO DE LARES.

REAL CEDULA [or Cédula Real]. An official document issued by the king, or in his name. The cédulas were the means for publishing and promulgating laws, decrees, and pronouncements. One type of royal cédula granted special personal privileges and favors.

REAL SOCIEDAD ECONOMICA AMIGOS DEL PAIS [or Real Sociedad Economica Amantes de la Patria] see SOCIEDAD ECONOMICA AMIGOS DEL PAIS

REGLAMENTO DE JORNALEROS see LA LIBRETA

REPARTIMIENTO. The Spanish system of allotting Indians to colonists as slave labor. The first repartimiento in Puerto Rico was made by Juan Cerón in late 1509.

RESIDENCIA. A type of public investigation of outgoing government officials during the Spanish colonial period. A "juez de residencia," or judge, was appointed for this purpose and he heard complaints and charges against even high officials such as the governor.

RESIDENT COMMISSIONER. The elected official who represents Puerto Rico before the U. S. Congress (House), with voice but not vote. This office was established by a provision of the First Organic Act of 1900. Recently the U. S. House granted the Commissioner the right to vote in House Committees of which he is a member. The Commissioner-elect (1973) is Jaime Benítez. See following entry.

RESIDENT COMMISSIONERS (to Washington, D. C.).
Federico Degetau 1900-1904.
Tulio Larrinaga 1905-1910.
Luis Muñoz Rivera 1911-1916 (died during his term).
Félix Córdova Dávila 1917-1932.
José Luis Resquera 1932-1933.
Santiago Iglesias Patín 1933-1939.
Bolívar Pagán 1940-1944.
Jesús F. Piñero 1945-1946 (appointed governor, 1946).
Antonio Fernós Isern 1947-1964.
Santiago Polanco Abreu 1965-1968.
Jorge L. Córdova Díaz 1969-1972.
Jaime Benítez 1973- .

REYES CORREA, ANTONIO DE LOS, ?-1758. "El Capitán Correa" was noted for his valiant efforts in defense of Arecibo, when the English attacked the town in August, 1702.

RIBERA [or Aldehuela]. Small village; usually consisting of an Indian settlement (ranchería) and the accompanying Spanish colonizers.

RICE. It was brought by Columbus to the Antilles on his second voyage and soon became acclimated. In 1783 the harvest in Puerto Rico was over 1000 tons, much of it grown along the west coast. The 1935 production of rice amounted to some 2, 450 tons. It later declined rapidly and has completely disappeared as an agricultural product, being completely imported.

RINCON. Municipio founded in 1770, along the northwest coast. Its location affords some of the highest waves and best surfing in the Atlantic or Caribbean. Area: 14 square miles. Population: 9, 094.

RIO GRANDE. Municipio to the east of San Juan, founded in 1840. Its accessibility to San Juan has produced a rapid growth of light industry and manufacturing. Meanwhile the agriculture sector, which generated 62% of income in 1950, now accounts for less than 5%. Area: 61 square miles. Population: 22, 032.

RIO PIEDRAS. Formerly an independent municipio, it was combined with San Juan in 1951. It was founded in 1714, on the site formerly known as El Roble. Today Río Piedras is most noted as the location of the largest campus of the University of Puerto Rico. See also UNIVERSIDAD DE PUERTO RICO.

RIVERS. The island's abundant rainfall and mountainous terrain have created an abundance of rivers, none of which are navigable by large boats, however. They are economically important as a source of hydroelectric power and water reservoirs. Among the principal rivers are the Yagüez, Grande, Guajataca, Coanillas, Bayamón and Loiza. Flooding of these rivers is common during the rainy season, May through November.

RODRIGUEZ CALDERON, JUAN, 1780-1840. Spanish poet who moved to Puerto Rico in 1802. He was among the first of the 19th-century poets.

RODRIGUEZ DE TIO, LOLA, 1843-1924. Poet and woman of revolutionary ideals. She came into conflict with the Spanish authorities when she wrote "subversive," inflammatory lyrics for "La Borinqueña," the danza which became the national anthem. See also LA BORINQUEÑA.

LA ROGATIVA. Legend holds that during the English assault on San Juan in 1797, the women of the city held a prayer vigil (rogativa), imploring Saint Ursula and the Eleven Thousand Virgins to liberate the city. The legend thus attributes the British withdrawal to this vigil. A statue by Lindsay Daen, "La Rogativa," was recently erected near San Juan harbor to commemorate these events.

ROSSY, MANUEL F., 1860-1932. Lawyer, politician and journalist. He once held the post of president of the insular House of Representatives.

RUIZ BELVIS, SEGUNDO, 1829-1867. A fervent abolitionist, he freed the slaves he had inherited. In 1886 he became a member of the Spanish Commission for Ultramarine Reforms, while the following year he was forced into exile when he denounced the colonial regime. He was a revolutionary and close ally of Betances. He died somewhat mysteriously in Chile, after having gone there to seek help for the independence revolution he was to take part in in 1868.

RUIZ RIVERA, JUAN, 1846-1924. A native of Mayagüez, he joined the Cuban revolutionary movement in New York in 1868. He led Cuban military units in 1868-78, in struggles against the Spanish regime. Ruiz held high government posts under the American military government of liberated Cuba. Then, under the first Cuban President, Tomás Estrada Palma, he was named to several positions, including Secretary of Treasury.

- S -

SABANA GRANDE. Municipio founded in 1813-1814, by Pedro Acosta. Located in the semi-arid southwest, it is generally a poor area economically, with sugar cane the main crop. Area: 37 square miles. Population: 16, 343.

SAEZ Y ALDAO, PABLO, 1827-1879. Poet and lawyer. He was one of the group of students in Barcelona studying during the mid-19th century, who contributed to works such as the Album Puertorriqueño. He became Dean of the College of Lawyers, and member of the Provincial Parliament.

SAGASTA PACT. A pact agreed upon in 1897 by a commission of the Autonomist (Liberal) Party, headed by Luis Muñoz Rivera, and Praxedes Mateo Sagasta, leader of the Spanish Liberal Party. It called for the Puerto

Rican party to be fused with the Spanish party, and to support its policies both in Spain and the Antilles. In exchange, Sagasta's Liberal Party agreed to grant maximum autonomy possible to the Antilles when Sagasta became prime minister. This promise included complete local freedom and equal rights with peninsular Spaniards. Backers of the pact in Puerto Rico saw autonomy as the only real possibility, with no hope for a republican government in Spain. The agreement caused a split in the Puerto Rico Liberal Party. When Sagasta was asked to form a government in Spain in October 1897, the agreement was kept and the Carta Autonómica for the Antilles was approved in November. See also CARTA AUTONOMICA DE 1897.

SALCEDO, DIEGO. A Spanish soldier, who in 1511 was drowned by the Indians as a test of the Spaniards' immortality. Seeing that the Spaniards were not gods, the Indians soon rose up in rebellion. See also INDIAN REBELLION.

SALINAS. Municipio on the south coast. Its cabecera is on the Caribbean. It officially became an independent town in 1851. Area: 69 square miles. Population: 21, 837.

SAMA Y AUGER, MANUEL MARIA, 1850-1913. An author of varied forms, including poetry, prose, drama and bibliography. At one time he directed the Ateneo Puertorriqueño, which in 1887 chose to reward him for his publication, Bibliografía Puertorriqueña.

SAN BLAS DE COAMO. One of the few early colonial communities of any substantial population. See also COAMO.

SAN GERMAN. Historic municipio, southwest of Mayagüez. The original settlement, founded in 1511 by Miguel de Toro, was located to the north along the coast. It was destroyed, however, by frequent French pirate raids, in 1528, 1530 and 1540. The remaining inhabitants, under the leadership of Simón de Osívar, were then granted a new town by a decree of the Audiencia of Santo Domingo in May 1570. Later, in 1573, a second decree had to be issued since the governor had failed to carry out the first one. The new town was to be called Nueva Villa de Salamanca, but the residents soon changed it to New San Germán, and later, simply San Germán.

SAN JUAN. The island's most populous municipio, its cabecera, which is the capital, was founded in 1521. It is thus the second oldest capital city in the hemisphere. The original city "Old San Juan," is well preserved and serves as an attraction to tourists, with its massive fortifications, historic churches, and blue-brick narrow streets. During the 16th century, San Juan was a departure point for Spanish exploration and colonization, and its location also was a strategic military site in the Caribbean. In 1647 Felipe IV called it "the key and vanguard of all the West Indies." Among the major fortifications are El Morro Fort begun in 1539, the city wall, begun in the 1630's, and Fort San Cristóbal, built in 1765. By the mid-19th century San Juan was totally fortified, with its defenses covering 266 acres, the walled portion covering some 62 acres. Today the municipio itself covers 47 square miles and has a population of 463, 242. Greater San Juan, on the other hand, is a sprawling urban mass of between 800, 000 and 900, 000 persons in an area of some 200 square miles. This includes the municipios of Cataño, Guaynabo, Bayamón, Carolina, Trujillo Alto and Toa Baja. It is by far the dominant "city" of the island.

SAN JUAN GATE. A large portal built about 1635, adjacent to La Fortaleza, and part of the defensive walls complex. The gate became the principal entrance from the sea to the old city.

SAN LORENZO. Municipio in the southeast, tobacco-producing region. Area: 53 square miles. Population: 27, 755.

SAN SEBASTIAN. Municipio. The original settlement, founded in 1752, was called Pepino. The present name, that of the town's patron saint, was adopted in 1869. Area: 71 square miles. Population: 30, 157.

SANTA CLARA, ANTONIO DE. One of Puerto Rico's first chroniclers. He participated in the preparation of a historically valuable description of the island in 1582. See also MEMORIA DE MELGAREJO.

SANTA CRUZ [or St. Croix]. The largest of the U. S. Virgin Islands, it was discovered by Columbus in 1493, just prior to the discovery of Puerto Rico. The Spanish Crown had thus long laid claim to it, but in conflicts with other European powers it was unable to maintain control. After the French sold the island to Denmark in 1733 the Spaniards again had plans to retake it. With a large force of men and ships, an expedition was sent in late 1734. When it arrived it did not attack, for lack of a royal order from the king. See also ST. CROIX, in the Virgin Islands section of this Dictionary.

SANTA ISABEL. Municipio whose cabecera is on the south coast. It became a town in 1842. Area: 34 square miles. Population: 16, 056.

SANTURCE. An urban barrio of San Juan. See also CANGREJOS, SAN MATEO DE.

SANZ, JOSE LAUREANO. Governor, 1868-1870. He founded the National Guard in December, 1869, due to his fear that the existing popular militia was untrustworthy. Two militia officers had been involved in the Lares Insurrection of 1868. See also GUARDIA NACIONAL.

LOS SECOS Y MOJADOS. A secret society of liberal criollos active in the year 1887. It was also known as "La Torre del Viejo." Several such groups were active at this time, and they were strongly attacked and persecuted for their autonomist-separatist views. See also EL COMPONTE.

SEIJO, SANTIAGO, 1840-1914. Physician and activist liberal political leader. As a strong supporter of justice and liberty for Puerto Ricans he was thus suspect by the Spanish authorities. He was arrested and jailed following the Grito de Camuy. See also GRITO DE CAMUY.

SERRALTA, BERNABE DE, 1530-1598. Heroic military officer who is noted for his valiant efforts to defend the capital during the attack of the English in 1598. The larger English forces under Clifford finally won out, Serralta being killed in the battle.

SEVENTEENTH CENTURY. This century was nearly devoid of any development in Puerto Rico. The island was forgotten by Spain, gold and Indians having disappeared, and the population remained small because of attacks by pirates and foreign powers, along with vicious hurricanes. In one report by a 17th-century governor it stated that by 1662 some 11 years had passed since a merchant ship from Spain had visited the island. To make matters worse, foreign commerce continued to be prohibited by Spain.

SEVERO QUIÑONES, JOSE, 1838-1909. After a career of public service, in 1900 he was named by President McKinley the first Chief Justice of the Puerto Rican Supreme Court.

SIGLO DE ORO. The 19th century is sometimes referred to as Puerto Rico's "Golden Century." Compared to the two previous centuries of relative stagnation, it represented a flourishing of commerce, wealth and particularly the arts, letters, and political liberalism.

SIERRA DE LUQUILLO. A mountain range in eastern Puerto Rico. Sparsely populated, it covers some 2.4% of the land area of the country. It is an area of "monadnocks," covered with exuberant vegetation. Excessive rainfall here, an average of 135 inches per year, has created the famous El Yunque rain forest.

EL SITUADO. An annual grant of funds by the Spanish colonial authorities from the rich Mexican treasury to sustain Puerto Rico. The first Situado came in 1766, and gradually increased to some 225 million pesos annually. By a royal order of 1784, the grant was reduced to 100,000 pesos annually until its termination in 1810. A total of some five million pesos were granted by the Situado. This allotment was needed because of the high cost of military fortifications built in Puerto Rico, combined with the meager, economically poor population. As late as 1776 the population totalled only some 76,000.

SLAVERY. The importation of African slaves into the island to replace the Indians who were rapidly extinguished, began in 1521. Puerto Rico even became a distribution center for slaves; but substantial slave importation did not begin until much later. The total number of slaves imported is estimated at only 77,000 of which some 75% were imported between 1808 and 1865. Unlike most other Caribbean islands, the white population was not outnumbered by slaves or free blacks, and even today, despite widespread racial mixing, the population is much "whiter" than on other Caribbean islands (except Cuba). Agitation for the abolition of slavery became heated in the mid-19th century. In 1865 the Spanish Abolition Society was created. Partial abolition began in June 1870, with total abolition decreed March 22, 1873. At that date about 29,000 negro slaves existed, 15,000 men and 14,000 women; some 75% were between the ages of 12 and 50.

SMUGGLING. Between the 16th and early 19th century it was a prominent factor in the economy, stimulated by the strong restrictions against free trade imposed by Spain. Even several governors and bishops publicly acknowledged its necessity, while many officials aided contraband trade. Smuggling declined rapidly in the 19th century after Charles III authorized free trade. Before this, nearly all trade between Spain and the New World passed through Seville, until 1715 when Cádiz was opened. After 1772, some eight ports in Spain and 32 in the New World were authorized, but it was the 1800's before trade with foreign countries was allowed.

SOBERAO. The floor of the house. It is a corruption of the Spanish word "sobrado."

SOCIEDAD ECONOMICA AMIGOS DEL PAIS. This society's purpose was to stimulate development of industry, trade, agriculture and the teaching profession. It's creation was authorized by a law of the Cortes of November 29, 1811. It was actually established under the leadership of Intendent Alejandro Ramírez in November, 1813. In the 1820's it sponsored the establishment of several college professorial positions. Throughout its history it actively promoted the progress and economic development of the island. It was abolished in 1898 with the arrival of the United States government.

SOCIEDAD FILARMONICA. The philharmonic society was founded in 1848 by Augustín Bouijois, who in the same year established a music academy and a school of French. During this period a large number of establishments for advanced studies were founded.

SOLER Y MARTORELL, CARLOS, 1855-1917. Especially versed in astronomy, Soler was also a lawyer, economist, politician and writer.

SOTOMAYOR, CRISTOBAL DE, ?-1511. One of the important early colonists, he once held the title of Alcalde Mayor. The king had given him an important concession; the granting of the best cacique of the Indians and a large land-holding. In 1511 he was killed in the Indian rebellion of that year, along with some 50% of the Spanish colony.

STAHL, AGUSTIN, 1842-1917. First Puerto Rican naturalist and prominent man of science. Physician and outstanding investigator of his time, classifying thousands of the island's flora and fauna.

SUGAR CANE. Cane was introduced from Santo Domingo in the early 16th century. By 1582 there were already 11 mills ("ingenios") but a decline then set in and by 1646 there were only seven mills in operation. Rapid growth of the sugar industry occurred after 1900, with large investment of U. S. capital, a protected market, and other aids from the U. S. While production was 81, 000 tons in 1900, by 1934 it had risen to 1. 1 million tons. Little growth was experienced thereafter; in fact a rapid decline set in by the 1960's. Today its very existence as a viable crop is threatened, despite the fact that it still provides 30, 000 to 40, 000 jobs. The few mills still in operation are nearly all government-owned and a $100 million government investment to revive the crop has thus far shown little prospect of success. Latest harvest was less than 250, 000 tons.

- T -

TADEO DE RIVERO, FRANCISCO, ?-1854. Educator, philanthropist and public servant of San Juan. He served as regidor in the San Juan city council, backing measures to help the poor and orphan children. He published an excellent manual for teachers on the education of children.

TAINO INDIANS. When the Spaniards arrived in 1493 it is estimated that some 70, 000 Taino Indians, a branch of the Arawak tribe, inhabited what they called the island of Boriquén. Like the other Arawaks they were noted for their peaceful nature, in contrast to the fierce, war-like Carib Indians which frequently attacked them and made them prisoners. The ruling class nobility of the Arawaks was called "nitaynos, " so it is probable that this was the origin of the Spanish word Taino. The Indians would have considered the arriving Spaniards in this category, and called them by this name. During 16th-century colonization of Boriquén, the Tainos were nearly exterminated by disease, forced labor, wars and flight to other islands. They never recovered from this 16th-century disaster and today's Puerto Rican population shows no traces of the Indian racial strain. However, their imprint is clearly seen in some customs, relics, and especially in place names.

TAPIA Y RIVERA, ALEJANDRO, 1827-1882. Among the leading 19th-century writers, he was a poet, historian and novelist. While in exile in Spain he compiled and edited Biblioteca Histórica de Puerto Rico, a valuable collection of documents from the 15th to the 17th centuries. As a political liberal Tapia emphasized the need to redeem his country through improved education.

TAPON. A traffic jam; congestion of automobiles.

TENIENTE A GUERRA. Head of a local militia unit. When military governments were implanted by Spain, as they were periodically, these officials assumed the positions of mayors. See also ALCALDE MAYOR.

EL TIEMPO. A newspaper founded in 1907 by José Celso Barbosa. It was the organ of the Partido Republicano.

TOA ALTA. Municipio founded in 1751, to the west of San Juan. In the early 16th century, settlers came here from the Spanish Canary Islands. It became the leader in agriculture and the site of Puerto Rico's first Agricultural Experiment Station, established in the early 16th century. Area: 27 square miles. Population: 18, 964.

TOA BAJA. Municipio; its cabecera was founded in 1745. It is currently an area of rapid population growth. Area: 24 square miles. Population: 46, 384.

TOBACCO. A crop indigenous to the Antilles, its cultivation was not begun until the 1620's because its free cultivation was not permitted until after a royal cédula of 1614. (Production had previously been prohibited, since in Europe it was considered a vice, or even a crime.) The peak year of production was reached in 1927 when some 50 million pounds were harvested. While the crop then declined it has been revived in recent years and today is second only to sugar cane in value of its harvest.

TODD Y WELLS, ROBERTO H., 1862-1955. St. Thomas-born politician, lawyer and writer. He was one of the founders of the Partido Republicano Puertorriqueño. He also held the position of secretary of the Puerto Rican Revolutionary Directorship in New York.

LA TORRE DEL VIEJO see LOS SECOS Y MOJADOS

TORRES VARGAS, DIEGO DE, 1590-1649. Canon lawyer and chronicler of the 17th century. His descriptive history of Puerto Rico, written in 1647, may be considered the first attempt at a documented, historical synthesis of the island.

TRAVIESO, MARTIN J. A 19th-century man of letters and politician. In the 1840's he was one of the contributors to the Aguinaldo Puertorriqueño.

TREATY OF PARIS. The peace treaty ending the short, Spanish-American War of 1898. The treaty was initially signed December 10, 1898; it was approved by the U.S. Senate and the President on February 6, 1899. The United States thus began its colonial involvement, while Spain lost the last remnants of its empire--Cuba, Puerto Rico and the Philippine and other Pacific Islands. In exchange the U.S. paid Spain the sum of $20,000,000. Especially significant for Puerto Rico's political future, the treaty provided that its political condition and the rights of its inhabitants were to be determined by the U.S. Congress.

TRUJILLO ALTO. Municipio in the metropolitan San Juan area. It attained "pueblo" status in 1801. Area: 21 square miles. Population: 30,669.

TUGWELL, REXFORD G., 1891- . The last American to occupy the post of governor of Puerto Rico. After devoting his early career to the academic world Tugwell entered public life as an adviser to presidential candidates. In the New Deal team of President Franklin D. Roosevelt, Tugwell became one of the outstanding figures as well as the most controversial. After his appointment as governor in 1941, he began to work closely with the new reform-minded Popular Party administration, under Luis Muñoz Marín. He introduced many of the administrative reforms so important in the 1940's development and transformation of Puerto Rican society.

TUNA, SAN ANTONIO DE LA. An 18th-century town which is presently the site of Isabela municipio. See also ISABELA.

- U -

UBARRI, PABLO. Head of the Unconditional Spanish Party in Puerto Rico in the late 19th century. At a time when many liberal, autonomous leaders were active, Ubarri urged unconditional support for Spanish policies. His reactionary stance included opposition to establishing a university on the island and equating any autonomous or reformist stance as equivalent to complete separatism.

UNITED STATES-PUERTO RICO COMMISSION ON THE STATUS OF PUERTO RICO. A commission established by the U. S. Congress in 1964, for the purpose of studying all the factors of the Commonwealth relationship. It was composed of seven members from the U. S. and six from Puerto Rico. After holding extensive hearings on the status question a final report was issued in July 1966. It recommended that a plebiscite be held on the status question. See also PLEBISCITE ON POLITICAL STATUS.

UNIVERSIDAD DE PUERTO RICO. A state-run university of several campuses founded in 1903. In the early 19th century the establishment of an institution of higher education was proposed to the Spanish parliament by the San Juan municipal government and the governor. By a disposition of March 4, 1823, installation of the University of Puerto Rico was approved. But the fall soon thereafter of the constitutional regime in Spain kept this from ever becoming a reality. Major changes in the organization of the university were made in the 1940's and again in the University Reform Law of 1966. There are now various autonomous campuses and a series of small regional two-year colleges, with the Council on Higher Education overseeing the system. The Council is composed of eight members appointed by the governor, the Secretary of Education being an ex-officio member.

U. P. R. see UNIVERSIDAD DE PUERTO RICO

UTUADO. Municipio in rural, central Puerto Rico founded in 1739. Area: 115 square miles. Population: 35, 494.

- V -

VALERO, ANTONIO, 1770-1863. A native of Fajardo, he became a distinguished military officer for Spain. Later, however, Valero grew disgusted with Spanish colonialism and was a leading figure in the Wars for Independence. He fought against the mother country in Mexico, Colombia and Peru, and had planned an expedition to the Antilles. Interestingly, Valero also possessed an almost unknown talent of his day, that of a ventriloquist.

VASALLO, FRANCISCO, 1823-1867. Popular doctor and poet. Studying medicine in Barcelona he became a member of the criollo circle which published the Album Puertorriqueño. His poetry had a naturalist emphasis.

VEGA ALTA. Municipio on the north coast founded in 1775. Its nearness to San Juan helps to attract much light industry to the area. Area: 28 square miles. Population: 22, 810.

VEGA BAJA. Municipio on the north coast, founded in 1776. As a village, it is known as El Naranjal. In 1972 it gained international notoriety as the site of the Mar y Sol Pop Festival. Area: 47 square miles. Population: 35, 327.

VELLON. A coin of five or ten cents. The U. S. nickel is known as a "vellón de cinco;" the dime is a "vellón de diez."

VENEZUELA'S INTERVENTION. During the early 19th-century Wars for Independence, countless rumors of expeditions to liberate Puerto Rico circulated. On at least two separate occasions actual invasions of the island by Venezuelan-based forces were carried out, both without success. In January 1816, a small force landed at Fajardo but was quickly forced out. In mid-1825, several Venezuelan ships landed at Punto Borinquén, on the northeast tip of the island, taking charge of a fort there. However, as in 1815, their initial success was repelled by Spanish forces and no Puerto Rican separatists were able to aid in the battle, due to their lack of organization. See also BOLIVAR, SIMON.

VIDARTE, SANTIAGO, 1827-1848. A young poet who already had created quite an impression before his death at age 21. While he lacked his own unique style, he was often romantic and showed a bright imagination.

VIEQUES ISLAND. Offshore island municipio of Puerto Rico. It is located between Puerto Rico and the Virgin Islands. Its early inhabitants were fierce Carib Indians, who often plagued the newly established Spanish settlements in Puerto Rico. In its early days the island was known as Crab Island. Its cabecera is Isabel Segunda, named after the Spanish Queen. Today the island is an economically depressed area. A large U. S. Naval base occupies much of the island. Area: 52 square miles. Population: 7, 767.

VILLALBA. Municipio; it attained this status in 1917. Area: 37 square miles. Population: 18, 733.

VIRGEN DE LA MONSERRATE. Our Lady of Monserrate is a famous shrine located in the town of Hormigueros in western Puerto Rico. Legend has it that in the 17th century a peon was attacked by a wild bull, and was saved by the appearance of the Virgin. The news of the miracle spread quickly, as did pilgrimages to the place of the vision. Later, about 1640, the peasants who had moved to the place to make their homes, built a church in her name. Pilgrimages have continued to the present, taking place annually on September 2.

VIZCARRONDO Y CORONADO, JULIO L. DE, 1830-1899. Newspaperman and writer. He founded one of the earliest political papers, El Mercurio, in 1837. At the beginning of January 1850, he was exiled from the island for his liberal, abolitionist ideas. After taking refuge in the United States he increased his anti-slavery stance. Later in life he became involved in politics in Madrid, defending Puerto Rican autonomy.

W: no entries

- X -

XIMENEZ PEREZ, MANUEL, ?-1781. A Spanish monk from the monastery Santa María la Real de Nájera. He was made Bishop of Puerto Rico in 1770, taking possession of the Cathedral in 1772. Two of his important accomplishments were the rebuilding of the Episcopal Palace and construction of a hospital for the poor of San Juan. This later project led to a severe conflict with Governor Dufresne. During a period of war with the English, Ximénex had loaned the hospital to the governor, who later refused to return it.

XIORRO Y VELAZCO, MIGUEL, 1743-1801. One of San Juan's earliest philanthropists and promoters of education. Inheriting great wealth, he later joined a religious order, living modestly. At his death Xiorro willed his fortune to education. The rents from his properties were also willed to the construction of a religious seminary and scholarships for poor students.

- Y -

YABUCOA. Municipio on the southeast coast, officially founded in 1793. Its name is derived from an Indian word meaning "the place of the yuca." Area: 55 square miles. Population: 30, 165.

YAGÜECA. The site of the decisive battle between the Spanish forces under Ponce de León, and the indigenous Taino Indians which had been in rebellion in 1511. See also INDIAN REBELLION.

YAÑEZ PINZON, VICENTE, ?-1514. The first person granted the right to colonize Puerto Rico, by the Spanish crown in 1510. He never carried out this task, merely touching at the island briefly, and so lost the right to this concession. He had captained the Niña on Columbus' first voyage to America. In 1500 he brought the first gold from Boriquén to the king.

YAUCO. Municipio. The town's creation was approved by a royal order of 1756. Area: 68 square miles. Population: 35, 103.

YOCAHU [or Yocahua]. Supreme god of the Taino Indians who were the indigenous people of Puerto Rico.

YUCA see CASABE

YUKIYU. God of the forces of good in the Taino Indian religion. He was supposed to reside on top of El Yunque, the popular name for the Luquillo Mountain range in northeast Puerto Rico.

EL YUNQUE. One of the highest mountain peaks, located in the Sierra de Luquillo, it reaches nearly 3, 500 feet. Here is located a tropical rain forest, with rainfall amounts reaching 180-200 inches per year. See also SIERRA DE LUQUILLO.

- Z -

ZENO GANDIA, MANUAL, 1855-1930. Novelist, poet, newspaperman, historian and physician. His novels brought Puerto Rican literature into the current of naturalism and carried Zeno Gandía to a high position among Hispanoamerican novelists. He was a founder of the Partido Union and also a militant in the Liga de Patriotas. In this latter role, along with Henna and Hostos, he went on a mission to Washington in 1898, demanding a solution to the political status of Puerto Rico.

<u>Addendum</u> (See p. 60)

NOCHE DEL JUA. "Judas Rides" celebrated by some residents of Isabela, Quebradillas and Camu y municipios to close Holy Week. Reportedly going back three centuries they are held to symbolize the punishment of Judas for his betrayal of Christ. After the pre-Easter Sunday midnight mass blindfolded horses with the effigy of Judas on their backs were set loose. People then chased the horses beating the effigies with sticks. In recent years, however, the celebration degenerated into a violent race in which the animals were beaten to death. Ordinances prohibiting the festivities and an educational program among the communities have been implemented in recent years and it appears that the practice will come to an end.

HISTORICAL DICTIONARY OF THE U. S. VIRGIN ISLANDS

ADAMS, ALTON AUGUSTUS, 1889- . Composer, Navy band leader (retired), journalist, and teacher, Adams was the first black conductor in U. S. Navy. In 1917 he composed the music for "Virgin Islands March," which is now the official song of the islands. A self-taught musician, he and his band served as liaison between the naval government and people of the Virgin Islands. Adams thus became closely associated with and the confidant of the naval governors. He also served as Associated Press correspondent and editor of his own newspaper for a time. He was president of the Virgin Islands Hotel Association for 19 years.

ALIENS. With the tourist and economic boom of 1960's there came a vast influx of alien workers, mainly from British islands. By 1968 some 45% of work force (95% of construction and 60% of service jobs) was alien. It is also estimated that over 70% of all Virgin Islanders were once aliens or stem from alien backgrounds. While supposedly "temporary" bonded workers, many "aliens" in fact are permanent residents.

AMALIENBORG. Official Danish name of Charlotte Amalie, St. Thomas. Until American purchase in 1917 this name was frequently used in official publications. See also CHARLOTTE AMALIE.

ATHENAEUM. A library-oriented institution established in St. Thomas in 1839. By 1851 it had some 121 members, mostly the wealthy and elite of St. Thomas, and 5,000 books in its library.

ARCHITECTURE. The town houses typical of Danish construction were based on the simple Danish pavilion. The construction was commonly based on a half-timbered building, with pillars, guiders and panelling.

AYAY [also Ay Ay; Iaha; Agay]. The name the Indians used to designate the island of St. Croix at the time of Columbus' arrival. These Indians were referred to as Ayayanos.

- B -

BAA, ENID MARIA, 1911- . Librarian, bibliographer and Caribbean scholar, she was the first, and for many years, the only woman in the Cabinet of Virgin Islands Governor. She is the chief librarian of Virgin Islands Libraries and a specialist in Caribbean history.

BAMBOULA. Drum dances of the West Indian Negroes. Common until about 1865 in St. Thomas, when street masquerading began to replace it. African in origin, the name is related to "bamboo," of which the drum was made.

BARENTZEN, ALINS VAN. World renowned concert pianist. The daughter of St. Croix-born parents, she has received honors from the French government and has played under several famous conductors.

BASKETRY. Traditional native basket-making talents were chiefly used for fisherman's baskets. A native tropical vine, called locally "basket wiss" or "hoop vine," was used. The French Chachas also did basket weaving but were especially craftsman of straw hats. See also CHACHAS.

BASSIN. Colloquial name for city of Christiansted, St. Croix. In French, Dutch, and Danish "Bassin" signifies basin, dock, or harbor. Its usage is uncommon today. The city presently (1970) has a population of 3020. Creoles distinguished Bassin from "Westend"--the term denoting town of Frederiksted.

BECKER, CAPTAIN FREDERICK GUSTAVE, 1842-?. Born in Kassel, Germany, he went to St. Thomas in 1877 after extensive navigation and sailing studies. An important figure in the Hamburg American Shipping Line, which was significant in the West Indies of this period. He also served as German consul in the Virgin Islands.

BEHN, SOSTHENES, 1882-1957. St. Thomas-born successful corporation executive and founder, president, and chairman of the Board of I. T. T.

BENJAMIN, AMOS RUDOLPH, 1876-1969. A dedicated civil servant, citizen soldier and church leader, in 1952 he was awarded the Royal Danish Medal of Merit by the Danish King in recognition of his life of public service under the Danes.

BENJAMIN, JUDAH P., 1811-1864. A native of St. Croix who held several posts in the Confederate Cabinet of Jefferson Davis, including Secretary of State and Minister of War. He was a world famous scholar, lawyer and politician and became a member of the Louisiana Legislature in 1842 and a Whig Presidential elector in 1848. Although highly unpopular with the Southern people, Benjamin had Jefferson Davis' firm confidence. In 1865 when the Confederacy collapsed, he escaped to England and was there admitted to the Bar to practice law.

BENYE. A fried puff made of banana and flour.

BENZTON, ADRIAN BENJAMIN, 1777-1827. Governor from 1816-1819 and an instrumental figure in the period of war with Britain, at the surrender of the Danes to the British in 1807 he is credited with obtaining favorable conditions regarding Danish matters. He once was married to the daughter of American millionaire John Jacob Astor. Benzton spoke several languages.

BI OR BY. A prefix placed before the name of an adult male person by a child, for instance, "Bi-Charlie."

BILL. A hooked, steel implement used to cut sugar cane.

BLACKBEARD'S CASTLE. The local name for Kiaer Tower, built on the summit of Government Hill, behind Fort Christian. While tradition says that this ancient tower overlooking St. Thomas was the abode of the pirate Blackbeard, history does not confirm this. Its thick walls and strategic location point out its defensive purpose. This structure was built even before Bluebeard's Castle, in 1674, by Karl Baggert; it was known as Fogarty Castle from 1800 to 1931, when it was purchased by Captain Thomas A. Kiaer. Much of the building adjoining the tower was destroyed by fire on December 2, 1952.

BLACKWOOD, CAPTAIN A. J. Born in Maine, he went from

being a poor, uneducated farmboy to St. Croix' leading businessman and sugar plantation manager in the 19th Century. He was a member of the Colonial Council, and a representative of the New York firm of Bartram Brothers which had vast holdings in St. Croix.

BLUEBEARD'S CASTLE. A tower for defense purposes built high above St. Thomas harbor by the Danish authorities in 1689 and used until 1735. Originally called Fredericks-fort, tradition rather than fact says that it was used by the famous pirate Bluebeard. It was sold to private owners in 1818.

BLYDEN, EDWARD WILMOT, 1832-1912. First black from the Virgin Islands to achieve wide distinction as scholar, linguist, teacher and friend of kings. He translated Christian and Islamic literature. He was educated in Liberia, since color prevented his acceptance at U. S. schools, and eventually became Liberian Secretary of State. He was described as a "champion of the Negro Race" for his extensive efforts throughout Africa on behalf of the Negro.

BORDEAUX [or Buddoe; Buddhoe], GENERAL (pseudonym) see GOTTLIEB, MOSES

BORNN, HUGO OWEN, 1902-1966. Musician, composer and educator. Born and raised in St. Thomas, he studied in New York and Paris and became a renowned organist and author of interesting arrangements of native folk songs.

BOUGH, JAMES A., 1905- . A lawyer, professor and legislator, on July 3, 1937 he became the first native to be named U. S. District Attorney for the Virgin Islands. From 1946 to 1954 he was chief of the Caribbean Section of the United Nations.

BOVE, PETER. An American from Vermont who was appointed by President Nixon to the post of Governor of the Virgin Islands in 1969. His nomination became very controversial and he was never confirmed by the Senate nor took office. Previously Bove had been comptroller for federal programs in the Virgin Islands.

BRANDENBURG AFRICAN COMPANY. In the late 17th century, Friederick Wilhelm, Elector of Brandenburg, and the Danish King agreed on establishing a factory and company plantation in the Virgin Islands. The previously established Danish West Indian Company had not been able to supply sufficient ships for slave and agricultural trade. The Brandenburg Company was so successful it took away business and even replaced tobacco with sugar cane production. The company was interested in selling its slaves to Spanish colonists, but the King of Spain refused direct importation into his West Indian ports and insisted on indirect dealing. Thus, in 1685 the Company negotiated a treaty with Denmark, and St. Thomas became a slave port and distribution point.

BREAKFAST CART. A small, swift mule cart which went to town daily for plantation supplies.

BREDAT, ERIC. He was elected Governor of St. Thomas for the years 1716 to 1724. St. John Island was developed and cultivated during his administration.

BRITISH OCCUPATION. In addition to 1801-1802 period (see TREATY OF AMIENS), the British occupied the Virgin Islands from December 22, 1807 to April 16, 1815 as well. Because of a crisis in British-French relations and France's friendship with Denmark, the British exchanged these Islands in 1815 for the Danish island of Heligoland.

BRITISH VIRGIN ISLANDS. In the contemporary period a nearly complete social and economic integration of these islands with the U. S. Virgin Islands has taken place. In 1969 the British Virgin Islands asked to be politically turned over to the United States, but extreme economic dependence makes this unlikely. The British Virgin Islanders are very dependent on jobs in St. Thomas, where they supply about 50% of the labor force. There is constant apprehension on the island due to a fear for a change in U. S. immigration policies.

BUKRA. Term used for white man, particularly the planter.

BUM OR BUMBA. The boss or driver of field hands on an estate, hence, the headman.

BURGHER COUNCIL. Founded about 1700, it was composed of some six representatives of the planters. Generally it lacked any real power to restrict the Governor or the Privy Council, which was determined by the Danish West India Company. The council's attempt to secure representative government was unsuccessful until about 1734 when the company yielded some of its preogatives. Its successor, the Colonial Council, was created by the King under the 1852 Colonial Law. It was called the Municipal Council from 1936 to 1954, under the First U. S. Organic Act for the Virgin Islands. Under the 1954 Revised Organic Act the Municipal Council became the Legislature.

- C -

CALYPSO. The origin of the name of the famed West Indian song remains a mystery. Natives of Trinidad claim it comes from their patois. It is basically slave music, expressing resentment and repugnance, that was originally sung by slaves enroute from Africa. Its popularity in part is due to variant forms of pronunciation of words and the accenting of wrong syllables.

CANE PIECE. Sugarcane field.

CANEGATA, D. C. Physician, legislator, and former judge, he was chief executive (administrator) of his native St. Croix.

CARENAGE. Suburb to the west of Charlotte Amalie where the French Chacha fishing community is centered. See also CHACHAS.

CARIB INDIANS. Fierce Indians which inhabited St. Croix when Columbus arrived in 1493. Carib Indian traces have been discovered at Magen Bay on St. Thomas and at Reef Bay on St. John. The last of these original inhabitants were eliminated by the Spaniards in the 16th Century.

CARUSO. A type of music used during Christmas and New Year.

CASTRO, MORRIS FIDANQUE, 1902-1966. First native Virgin Islander to hold the post of Governor under the U. S. flag (1950-1954). Born in Panama of Virgin Islander parents, Castro rose from the lowest ranks of government service.

CENSUS. It was first ordered taken by the Danish government in 1688 and was carried out by Frank Martins, A. Brock and Simon Luck. The total population then was less than 1000, the majority of which were Negro slaves. The population of Charlotte Amalie in 1688 was 35 whites and four slaves. Periodic Danish censuses taken of the islands show a steady growth of population during the 18th and 19th centuries, to a peak of 43, 178 in 1835, at which time the capital, Charlotte Amalie, was the third largest city in the Danish monarchy. Then followed a steady decline (beginning first in St. Croix) to a mere 26, 000 at time of U. S. purchase in 1917. The Virgin Islands experienced rapid growth during the 1960's and the official 1970 U. S. census showed 62, 468 people, a 94% increase over the 1960 census. The urban population actually declined 15% and the rural increased 235%. Many sources in the Virgin Islands dispute the 1970 census data and claim nearly 80, 000 residents, a disparity due to the presence of many unregistered aliens from nearby islands come to find employment.

CHACHAS. A white French ethnic enclave in St. Thomas, historically in the lower class economically but considered to be upper class in race and culture. The latter element has resulted in the group's present-day closed communities. Originally poor fishermen, basket makers and farmers, today many are successful in business and banking. The Chachas, Catholics, are descendents from colonists who came from Brittany and originally settled on St. Bartholomew island. About the mid-19th Century a group of these descendents migrated to St. Thomas in search of better economic opportunities.

CHARLOTTE AMALIE, 1650-1714. Danish Queen, wife of Danish King Christian V, at the time of Danish colonization in West Indies. Born in Kassel, Germany, she married the then Prince and later King Christian V in 1667. Her Reform religion at first was an obstacle as Lutheranism was the state religion.

CHARLOTTE AMALIE. The capital of St. Thomas and the seat of the U. S. Virgin Islands government. Founded in the 17th Century and developed as a shipping and trading center, it was greatly devastated by fire and hurricanes in the early 19th Century. The city's namesake is the Moravian missionary Princess Charlotte Amalie, who came to St. Thomas in 1672. The 1970 population was officially 12, 220.

CHRISTIAN, ALMERIS LEANDER, 1919- . St. Croix-born, he was the first Virgin Islander to be named Judge of U. S. Federal District Court of the Virgin Islands. President Nixon nominated him to this post in 1969.

CHRISTIAN IV, 1577-1648. Danish King who contributed to Danish colonial commercial ventures by sending expeditions to Greenland and establishing the East India Company.

CHRISTIAN V, 1646-1699. The Danish King who in 1671 authorized a charter for the Danish West India Company to colonize St. Thomas. His wife, the Queen, was former Princess Charlotte Amalie.

CHRISTIAN VII see FREDERICK VI

CHRISTIANSEN, VIGGO. A doctor, and one of the two representatives from the Virgin Islands before the Danish Parliament during 1916 hearings on possible sale to the U. S.

CHRISTIANSTED. The principal city of St. Croix, its population in 1970 was officially 3, 020--41% less than in 1960. The town came into existence in 1733, the year Denmark bought St. Croix from the French. It served briefly as the capital of the Danish West Indies. The population is currently about half Puerto Rican, originally imported cane-cutting laborers. See also BASSIN.

CHRISTMAS, CAPTAIN WALTER VON. An adventurous and somewhat scheming Danish citizen who sought to initiate new negotiations in 1899 between U. S. and Denmark over sale of Virgin Islands. Having been dismissed for his questionable conduct in the Navy, he sought to earn 10% commission on sale price by working unofficially for Denmark. Denmark wanted to avoid public negotiations because of a previous rebuff in 1860, so was willing to use his services.

CI OR CY. A prefix placed before the name of an adult female by a child; for instance, "Ci-Mary."

CITIZENSHIP. When U. S. took possession of the Virgin Islands in 1917 the people were not granted U. S. citizenship but rather the title, "inhabitants of the Virgin Islands entitled to the protection of the U. S." On February 25, 1927 Congress enacted the Citizenship Act, granting citizenship to those currently residing in Virgin Islands.

CLAUSEN, PETER, 1721-1784. A plantation owner and Governor of St. Croix from 1751 to 1755, Clausen enjoyed much recognition there. He accomplished restoration of Fort Christian and improved the defenses. He was governor of all three islands, 1766-1770 and 1773-1784.

COLLEGE OF THE VIRGIN ISLANDS. A modern small, four-year college located near Charlotte Amalie founded in the early 1960's. The first class graduated in 1965.

COLONIAL LAW OF THE DANISH WEST INDIA POSSESSIONS see COLONIAL LAW OF 1852

COLONIAL LAW OF 1852. Purchase of the Virgin Islands by the King from the Danish West Indian Company in 1754 brought certain changes in the judicial system and taxation; in addition there was a 1798 royal ordinance dealing with the "reconciling court." But the first Danish Colonial Law was not inacted until 1852. It created a colonial assembly council with "deliberative voice" regarding legislative powers; four members appointed by the King, eight elected from St. Croix, six from St. Thomas and two from St. John. There was limited suffrage: males over 25 with 500 dollars annual income or who paid property tax. On request of this council the King might decree two separate assemblies, one for St. Croix, another for St. Thomas and St. John. The basic new provision of this 1852 Colonial Law was directed at the complaints of the excessive power disposed by the governor. The 1852 law proved unsatisfactory and a second one was enacted in 1863.

COLONIAL LAW OF 1863. (See previous entry.) This law founded a colonial council with real legislative power, superseding the mere deliberative body conceived of in

1852. Further, the Governor was now to administrate the affairs of the municipality where he resided and a president and vice-governor were assigned to the other municipalities. A comprehensive Bill of Rights was also added. Many provisions of this law remained in force even after two decades of U. S. rule. Suffrage remained limited, however.

COLONIAL LAW OF 1906. This legislation amended the Danish Colonial Law of 1863 in some minor provisions, but for the most part represented a reenactment of the 1863 law.

COLONIZATION. Settlement began perhaps as early as 1625 in St. Croix and 1647 in St. Thomas--nearly 150 years after their discovery. Colonization of the Danish West Indies was attempted from 1666, but a permanent colony was not established until 1671 on St. Thomas. When the colony on St. Thomas was refounded in 1671 the number of settlers was very small. Of the 190 who left Denmark in early 1671, only 48 were living by Christmas of that year.

CONSTITUTIONAL CONVENTION OF 1964. The legislature of the Virgin Islands convened a special "con-con" in 1964, submitting new demands for self-government to Congress. Chiefly involved was the right to elect the governor and a delegate to Congress. The U.S. Congress passed the Elective Governor Act in 1968 and the first elected Governor took office on January 4, 1971.

COPENHAGEN COMPANY. The first Danish venture to the West Indies in 1666 was said to represent this company. The colony under Erik Smidt's leadership failed to establish itself, Smidt himself dying shortly after arrival.

COTTON. The chief product of the 17th Century, it reached its peak in St. Croix in 1797, when 151, 000 pounds were produced. During the U. S. Civil War cotton had a brief revival, but fell into insignificance rapidly.

COUNCILS. Under Danish rule, Claus Hansen established both the Privy ("Sekrite") Council and the Common ("Ordinary") Council in 1702. The Common Council became, 150 years later, the Colonial Council ("Kolonialraadene").

CRAB ISLAND. This island is known today as Vieques, an off-shore municipality belonging to Puerto Rico. The Danes claimed it unsuccessfully in the 17th Century and it remained in Spanish hands. It lies between Puerto Rico and St. Thomas. Area: 52 square miles (making it larger than St. Thomas). Population: 7817.

CRAMER, LAWRENCE WILLIAM, 1897- . American Governor of the Virgin Islands from 1935 to 1941, and Lieutenant Governor, 1931-1935. During his administration he signed and implemented the Organic Act of 1936. He was also Secretary General of the Caribbean Commission from 1946 to 1951.

CRONE, MIKKEL KNUDSEN, ?-1716. He was Governor in 1710-1716 and previously the Head Bookkeeper of the Danish West India Company and a high member of the Privy Council. He introduced a distinct Danish administration in the colony.

CROSSWITH, FRANK RUDOLPH, 1892- . A native of St. Croix, he became a prominent labor union organizer in the United States, pioneering in organizing Negro workers. He was vice-chairman of the first American Labor Party during La Follette's Presidential campaign.

CRUZIAN. A native of the island of St. Croix.

- D -

DA COSTA, JACOB MENDEZ, 1833-1900. A great teacher and clinician, whose medical writings were of outstanding quality. He was born in St. Thomas, but lived and studied in Europe and the United States. He became president of the Association of American Physicians in 1897.

DAILY NEWS. English-language newspaper founded August 1, 1930, by J. A. Jarvis and A. Melchoir. It is one of the leading papers in the country today.

DANISH WEST INDIA COMPANY. A corporation organized in 1671 for the purpose of developing a profitable trade with the mother country, and returning a profit for its investors. Its colonial operation in St. Thomas began almost immediately, later spreading to St. John, and in 1733 to St. Croix. The company lasted some 84 years, until purchased by the Danish King, in 1754. The company's start was highly influenced by Dutch merchants resident in Denmark, who in 1670 persuaded the Danish King of the profitable possibilities for Negro slave trade. The Danish West India Company was allowed to set up operations in Africa for procuring slaves, as well as a St. Thomas base of operations. The company was modeled after the Dutch West India Company. In 1674 its name became the Danish West India and Guinea Company.

DANNEBROG. The Danish flag; equivalent of the American Stars and Stripes.

DA POINCY, PHILIPPE DE LONVILLIERS. French aristocrat, adventurer and a high member of the Knights of Malta. His ruthless exploits in the Caribbean in the 17th Century included conquests on St. Kitts, St. Marten and finally St. Cruz. With a small force he booted out the Spanish Governor in 1650 and renamed the island St. Croix. This began a long period of Knights of Malta rule and French control until 1733.

DELAVIGNE, FRANZ [also: de la Vigne]. Appointed Governor of St. Thomas, 1692-1694 by Thormohlem, who then had a lease on the island. His ignorance of the colony's conditions brought unpopular reaction.

DRIP STONE. A large, hollow limestone which was used to filter water.

DRIVER. Foreman on a sugar estate.

DU BOIS. One of the French governors of St. Croix. Appointed in 1659, he held the position until approximately 1665.

- E -

EH EH. An exclamation denoting surprise, concern. Often followed by "Well, me God."

"THE ERIK." Name of the ship on which Captain Erik Smidt sailed to St. Thomas from Copenhagen 1665-1666 on the first Danish expedition to the West Indies.

ESANNASON, WILHELM. Reputed to be first Negro physician from the Virgin Islands.

ESMIT, ADOLPH. Governor of St. Thomas, 1682-1684. He was the younger brother of Nicolai Esmit (which see) and went to the Virgin Islands from England when his brother became governor. He became captain of a slave ship. He joined opponents of his brother and was himself appointed Governor in 1682. His administration was a scandalous time for the colony. He had been a buccaneer himself and he made St. Thomas a haven for runaway criminals and debtors. Pirates and buccaneers were also openly received, making St. Thomas a threat to the other West Indian colonies. England thus brought pressure on the Danish King for Esmit's removal.

ESMIT, NICOLAI. Governor of St. Thomas, 1680-1682, he was unique in that he applied for the governorship. During a revolt in 1682 his brother Adolph (which see) took command. Nicolai was jailed, pronounced insane and tried in Denmark.

EVANS, MELVIN HERBERT, 1917- . The current (1972) Governor of the Virgin Islands, he was appointed to the office in 1969 and later became the first elected Governor, January 4, 1971. He is a physician and the former Commissioner of Health. He was born in Christiansted, St. Croix.

- F -

FIREBUN. Rebel or rioter. A term used for those involved in the labor riot of 1878.

FLAG. The local flag of the Virgin Islands was adopted by executive order of Governor Kittelle in May 1921. On a white background are placed block letters "V. I." in blue, between which is an American Eagle displayed in yellow.

FLEMING, H. W., 1864-?. Of Irish stock, he was a self-made prominent businessman of 19th Century St. Croix and a member of the Colonial Council.

FORT BERG. A fort built by the first permanent Danish settlers on St. John. It was established in 1717 by some 20 planters and five soldiers, when the colony immediately began construction of a fort on the summit of a small peninsula known as Fort Berg Hill. It is in ruins today.

FORT CHRISTIAN. The oldest Danish fort in the islands, it was erected immediately after the arrival of the permanent colonization effort on St. Thomas of 1671. It contained the government offices, jail, Governor's residence and the Lutheran Church, erected in 1706. In 1793 the church was moved to a new site outside the fort. The original fort was a masonry tower structure; completely renovated in 1874, the fort is still used by the government.

FREDERICK VI, 1768-1839. As Regent during part of the reign of his father Christian VII (i.e., 1784-1808) because of the latter's insanity, he abolished the importing of slaves in 1803 (but the slaves then living were not emancipated until 1848).

FREDERIKSTED. The second most populous urban place on St. Croix island. Its population in 1970 was 1531. This represented a decline of 30% from the 1960 census.

FREE PORT. One of the stipulations in Denmark's transfer of the islands to the U.S. in 1917 was that they forever remain free ports, with no customs duties being collected. As early as 1774 the King of Denmark decreed that ships could stop in St. Thomas without paying a harbor fee. Their free port status has contributed greatly to the recent boom in tourism in the islands.

- G -

GEOGRAPHY. About 68 islands and cays are found in the American Virgin Islands. Only three have any size or population of importance: St. Thomas, St. Croix, and St. John, and the total land area of these three is only 132 square miles. Two-thirds of this area is St. Croix alone. The islands are located some 40 miles east of Puerto Rico and 1100 miles southeast of Miami, Florida. The highest point (in St. Thomas) is West Mountain, 1,515 feet. The islands are believed to have been part of a landmass once including Puerto Rico, Santo Domingo, Cuba, and Yucatan.

GARDELIN, PHILIP, ?-1740. He was Governor from 1733 to 1736, during the fierce slave revolt on St. John. His strict slave ordinance proclaimed in 1733 is blamed as one of the major causes of the revolt. See also SLAVE REVOLTS.

GOTTLIEB, MOSES. A young slave who was the secret organizer and avowed leader of the slave revolt on St. Croix in 1848. Known popularly as Buddoe, or General Bordeaux, he was a young Black from the British islands. When he and a band of followers threatened Frederiksted on July 4, 1848, they were met by the Danish authorities and promised abolition. The abolition was proclaimed by Governor von Scholten, whom many felt knew about the planned uprising and concurred with it. Buddoe was freed, but deported and set ashore in Trinidad, never to return to the Danish West Indies.

GOVERNMENT [under the U. S.] see ORGANIC ACT OF ...

GOVERNOR. The chief executive of the islands. A variety of foreign powers have appointed the governors in the Virgin Islands. Long under Danish rule, they were principally Danes from 1666 to 1917, except on St. Croix before 1733 and during brief British occupations in the early 19th Century. U. S. -appointed governors held office from 1917 until 1970. Historical records are often in conflict or confusing when listing the early Danish governors. This is due mainly to the fact that for some time, even under the Danish rule, two governors existed simultaneously, one in St. Thomas and the other in St. Croix. See the following two entries.

GOVERNORS OF THE VIRGIN ISLANDS. (Under Danish rule.)
Erik Nielsen Smidt: March 1666 to June 1666.
Jesper Hoyer 1666-1667.
Jorgen Iversen 1672-1680.
Nicolai Esmit 1680-1682.
Adolph Esmit 1682-1684.
Gabriel Milan 1684-1686.
Mikkel Mikkelsen 1686
Christopher Heinz 1686-1688.
Adolph Esmit 1688
Iver Hoppe 1688
Christopher Heinz 1688-1689
Johan Lorentz 1689-1692.
Franz Delavigne 1692-1694.
Johan Lorentz 1694-1702.

Claus Hansen 1702-1706.
Joachim (Jokum) Melchior v. Holten 1706-1708.
Diderich Mogensen 1708-1710.
Michel Knudsen Crone 1710-1716.
Erik Bredal 1716-1724.
Otto Jacob Thambsen 1724
Friedrick Moth 1724-1727.
Hemik Suhm 1727-1733.
Philip Gardelin 1733-1736. (During this period St. Croix was purchased from France, with formal possession taking place January 8, 1735. Seat of government of the three Virgin Islands was moved to St. Croix in 1748. After 1748, separate Governor General for all three islands, and Vice-Governor for St. Thomas and St. John together until 1862.)
Friedrick Moth, I: 1736-1744 (first Danish governor of St. Croix).
Christian von Schweder 1744-1747.
Christian Suhm 1747-1755.
Christian Lebrscht Baron von Prock 1755-1766.
Peter Clausen 1766-1770.
Friedrick Moth, II: 1770-1772
Ulrich Wilhelm Roepstorff 1765-1766.
Heinrich Ludwig Ernst von Schimmelmann 1773.
Peter Clausen 1773-1784.
Heinrich Ludwig Ernst von Schimmelmann 1784-1787.
Ernst Frederick von Waltersdorf 1787-1794.
Wilhelm Anton Lindermann 1794-1796.
Thomas de Malleville 1796-1798.
Wilhelm Anton Lindermann 1798-1801.
[First period of English Occupation: March 31, 1801 to February 16, 1802.]
John Clayton Powell 1801-1802.
Ernst Frederick von Waltersdorf 1802-1803.
Balthazar Frederik Muhlenfels 1803-1807.
Hans Christopher Lillienshjold 1807.
[Second English Occupation: 1807-1815.]
Henry Bowyer (Governor of St. Croix) 1807-1815.
McClean (General Commander in St. Thomas) 1807-1815.
Peter Lotharius Oxholm 1815-1816.
Johan Henrik von Stabel 1816.
Andrian Benjamin Benson 1816-1819.
Johan Henrik von Stabel 1819-1820.
Carl Adolph Rothe 1820-1822.
Johan Frederik Bardenfleth 1822-1827.
Peter Carl Frederik von Scholten 1827-1831.
Johannes Søbøther 1831-1832.
Peter Carl Frederik von Scholten 1832-1834.
Johannes Søbøther 1834-1835.

Peter Carl Frederik von Scholten 1835-1848.
Frederik von Oxholm 1848.
Peter Hansen 1848-1851.
Hans Ditmar Frederik Feddersen 1851-1855.
Johan Frederik Schlegel 1855-1860.
Wilhelm Ludwig Birch 1860-1871.
[Seat of Government returned to St. Thomas in 1871.]
John Christmas 1871.
Franz Ernst Bille 1871-1872.
Johan August Stahemann 1872.
Janus August Garde 1872-1876.
Carl Anton Frederik Christian Hattensen 1876.
Christian Henrik Arendrup 1881-1884.
Peter Mathias Simonsen Anderson 1884-1885.
Christian Henrik Arendrup 1885-1888.
Peter Mathias Simonsen Anderson 1888-1889.
Christian Henrik Arendrup 1889-1893.
Carl Emil Hedemann 1893-1903.
Herman August Jürs 1903-1904.
Frederik Martin Mortensen Nordlien 1904-1905.
Christian Magdalus Thestrup Cold 1905-1908.
Peter Carl Limpricht 1908-1911.
Lars Christian Helwig-Larsen 1911-1915.
Reimund Baumann 1915.
Lars Christian Helwig-Larsen 1915-1916.
Henri Konow 1916-1917.

GOVERNORS OF THE VIRGIN ISLANDS. (Appointed by U. S. Presidents.) (These were all Naval officers from 1917 to 1931.)
James Harrison Oliver 1917-1919.
Joseph Wallace Oman 1919-1921.
Sumner Ely Wetmore Kittelle 1921-1922.
Henry Hughes Hough 1922-1923.
Philip Williams 1923-1925.
Martin Edward Trench 1925-1927.
Waldo Evans 1927-1931.
Paul Martin Pearson (first civilian) 1931-1935.
Lawrence W. Cramer 1935-1941.
Charles Harwood 1941-1946.
William H. Hastie 1946-1949.
Morris Fidanque de Castro 1950-1954.
Archie Alexander 1954-1955.
Walter A. Gordon 1955-1958.
John David Merwin 1958-1961.
Ralph M. Paiewonsky 1961-1969.
Melvin Herbert Evans 1969- . (He is the first popu-

larly elected [November 1970] governor.)

GYLLICH, JACOB HEITMANN, 1795-1868. A major in the Danish garrison on St. Croix at the time of the 1848 slave revolt. He is credited with successfully working with slave leader Buddoe in avoiding bloodshed, restoring peace, and bringing abolition.

- H -

HAMILTON, ALEXANDER, 1755-1804. Famous American statesman and founding father. He was the first U.S. Treasury Secretary. Born in the British West Indies, he later moved to St. Croix. In 1772 he was an apprentice in an accounting house there.

HANSEN, CLAUS, ?-1706. Governor of the Danish West Indies, 1702-1706. He became a well-to-do plantation owner as his wife's heir. He had led the planters' opposition to local leadership before becoming Governor. Hansen organized the "Privy" and "Ordinary" Councils.

HANSEN, PETER, 1798-?. Holder of Governor General posts in both the Danish East and West Indies. Widely traveled in the Orient, Hansen established several consular offices in the Far East. After retirement in 1847 he accepted the post of Governor in the Danish West Indies, with the task of reorganizing the administration after the 1848 slave revolt.

HARRISON, HUBERT HENRY, 1883-?. An educator, writer and literary critic, he was born in St. Croix but left at age 19 for New York where he later made his fame. He founded and edited The Voice in 1917, edited the New Negro, and was a literary critic for The New York Times.

HEDEMANN, CARL EMIL, 1852-1929. He was Governor from 1893 to 1903, but also a famous party-giver. He called himself the "West Indies Innkeeper," and introduced the yearly feast Shrove-Monday into the Danish West Indies.

HEEGAARD, ANNE, 1790-1859. A free mulatto, she was the famed mistress of Governor von Scholten. She probably urged von Scholten to free the slaves. She was known as a woman of both wealth and experience. After emancipation of the slaves she reportedly cancelled a large debt owed to her by von Scholten.

HEINZ, CHRISTOPHER, ?-1689. A sergeant from Hamburg, Germany who arrived in St. Thomas in 1680, becoming head of Fort Christian. He later served as Acting Governor of St. Thomas from 1686 to 1688 and again briefly in 1689.

HILL, VALDEMAR ALEXANDER, 1914- . A St. Thomas legislator and local author, he is one of the organizers of the Progressive Guide, first Virgin Islands political party. He has also been a well-known labor organizer.

HODGE, WALTER J. M. A veteran legislator from St. Croix, he was President of the first, second, and fourth Legislative Assemblies.

HOYER, JESPER. Governor of St. Thomas from 1666 to 1667, having been appointed after the death of Erik Smidt. After his death in 1667 the first colonization effort failed, with no government of the colony until 1672.

HUNTUM. A Dutch governor who is credited with leading the assault on the St. Thomas settlement about 1667. Records indicate that this assault broke up the Danes' first colonization effort. No exact date is recorded for these events, but it would have been between 1667 and 1670.

HURRICANES. The Virgin Islands have been hit and damaged severely by hurricanes throughout their history. Since 1726, islanders have observed Supplication Day, a day set aside to ask for a peaceful hurricane season. The most recent devastating hurricanes were those of 1916, 1928 and 1932.

HUTSON, ARCHBISHOP EDWARD, 1873-1936. He was ordained as a priest in St. Thomas in 1896 and served that parish until 1903. He later rose through the church hierarchy to become Archbishop of the West Indies. In 1925 he was knighted by King George V. When the Danish Islands were transferred to the U. S., Hutson had his Virgin Island parishes placed under the jurisdiction of Puerto Rico.

- I -

INTER-VIRGIN ISLANDS CONFERENCE. As a result of the effort to establish closer ties between the British and American Virgin Islands, this Conference was established in 1951. It is under the joint chairmanship of the Governor of the U. S. Virgin Islands and the Commissioner of the British Virgin Islands.

IVERSEN, GEORGE JORGEN, 1638-1683. The first "official" Governor of St. Thomas, from 1672 to 1680. He took office upon initiation of the second, permanent, colonizing attempt by the Danes. He was murdered in 1683 while aboard the _Neptune._

- J -

JACKSON, DAVID HAMILTON, 1884-1946. St. Cruzian by birth, he was a noted judge, lawyer, politician and labor organizer. He fought for freedom of the press and organized the first labor union. Disillusioned by unfulfilled Danish promises of reform he led the fight to transfer the islands from Denmark to the U. S. However, in 1922, as a member of the Colonial Council, he went to Washington protesting against the U. S. Naval Government. In 1915 he began publishing _The Herald_, the first nongovernment-controlled newspaper.

JARVIS, JOSE ANTONIO, 1901-1963. A St. Thomas author, poet, teacher, philosopher and humanitarian. He made substantial contributions to the Virgin Islands and in 1930 founded the _Daily News._

JAW BONE. A native candy.

JEWS. From the beginning of Danish colonization, Jews have settled in St. Thomas. Many Jewish figures are prominent throughout the history of the Virgin Islands, including Governor Milan, one of the first governors. In 1814, by Royal Ordinance, Denmark became the first modern nation to pass laws for the protection and liberation of Jews.

- K -

KALALOO. A native soup made of greens and herbs, seasoned with ham, fish, conch and crab.

KING, CYRIL E., 1921- . For 12 years he was on the staff of Senator Hubert Humphrey. In 1961 President Kennedy appointed him as Government Secretary in the Virgin Islands, a post he held some eight years. During this period he disagreed strongly with Governor Paiewonsky and founded the Independent Citizens Movement to compete in the 1970 elections.

KINGO, JOHANNES CHRISTIAN. He was ordained as a missionary pastor in Christiansted in 1771 in the first, and only, such ordination in the Danish West Indies. He was also the first minister to the slaves on St. Thomas. In 1764 he translated Luther's "Small Catechism" into Dutch Creole, although it was not published until 1770 in Copenhagen.

- L -

LABAT, PIERRE. A Frenchman who visited the Danish West Indies at the beginning of the 18th century. His detailed account of this visit, published in 1722, gives a good description of the life, culture and architecture of St. Thomas of this period. Living for several years as a Dominican missionary in the West Indies he wrote lively contemporary accounts, especially of the buccaneers.

LABORER'S RIOT OF 1878. A destructive, violent riot of Negro laborers erupted in St. Croix in October 1878. After the 1848 emancipation, country laborers on plantations were still legally obligated to work under one-year contracts with strict provisions. Laborers thus complained that the Labor Act was merely a new kind of slavery, providing a 10-cent per day wage. Resentment finally led to mob violence with an attack on the Fort at Frederiksted. The mob's anger then turned to the burning and sacking of the town, especially the white merchants. Plantations were also burned and the city of Christiansted was threatened before reinforcements from St. Thomas and neighboring islands were able to put down the insurrection. Immediately thereafter the Labor Act was repealed.

LANSING, ROBERT, 1864-1928. U. S. Secretary of State who strongly urged the purchase of the Danish West Indies, believing them to have extensive military and commercial value. He signed the purchase agreement in 1916.

LEADER, RICHARD, 1889- . Noted criminal lawyer, orator, writer and champion of education and freedom of the press. Leader is a native of Christiansted. As Dean of the Virgin Islands Bar he is known as the "Clarence Darrow of his time."

LEGISLATURE. The present day (1972) Virgin Islands Legislature is unicameral, with 16 members called senators. Five are elected-at-large, while eleven senators are elected from three districts: five each from St. Thomas and St. Croix, one from St. John. The term of legislative office is two years; elections are held the first Tuesday in November.

LEIDESDORF, WILLIAM, 1810-1848. A St. Cruzian, he migrated to San Francisco in 1841 and there became very successful in business, acquiring wealth and fame. At his death he owned the largest estate in California.

LIGHTBOURNE, JOHN N. A newspaper editor and noted Virgin Islands historian.

LOCKHART, ALFRED H., 1862-1931. The Horatio Alger of the Virgin Islands. He began as a grocer's clerk and through shrewd business techniques became a millionaire. He was also a musician and politician.

LORENSEN, JOHN [or Lorentz, Johan], ?-1702. In 1688 he became a member of the Privy Council. Appointed Acting Governor at the death of Governor Heinz in 1689, he continued to hold the post during the period of Thormohlen's leasing of St. Thomas. He headed the establishment of the town next to Fort Christian. During a later term as Governor, 1694-1712, he strengthened the colony's defenses against the threats of several privateers, including the famed pirate Kidd.

LOW ROOT. Subtle rumor, especially as it applies to scandal or character defamation.

LUCCHETTI, SOSTHENES. A native of Toulose, France, he emigrated to St. Thomas as a youth in 1854. He became an accomplished linguist, statesman and noted intellectual. From 1870-1875 he was president of the Colonial Council, thereafter resigning to become French consul.

LUGO, RON DE, 1930- . Born in the U. S. and raised in Puerto Rico, he went to the Virgin Islands about 1950. He was elected in 1968 to represent Virgin Islands interests in Washington. As a lobbyist he is given much credit for the 1972 Congressional approval of a non-voting Resident Commissioner from the Virgin Islands. In 1959, at age 29, he became the youngest man ever elected National Committeeman for the Democratic Party of the U. S.

LUTHERANS. The first Lutheran congregation was established in 1666 by Slagelse. Since the Lutheran Church was Denmark's National Church, Lutherans have played prominent roles in Virgin Islands history.

- M -

MAAS, DAVID, E., 1914- . Lieutenant Governor of the Virgin Islands at present (1972). This post is second in rank to the governor. Until 1969 this post was called "Government Secretary."

MAGENS, JOACHIM MELCHOIR, I., c1715-1783. An 18th-Century St. Thomas scholar, he prepared a grammar of Dutch Creole in 1770 for use by missionaries studying the language.

MADURO, JOHN, 1921- . Attorney, legislator and current (1972) president of the Virgin Islands Legislature.

MALLEVILLE, THOMAS DE, 1739-1798. The first native-born Virgin Islands Governor. He was Governor of St. Thomas from 1793 to 1796. Originally, however, he had been appointed as Commandant on St. Thomas to preside in the Governor General's absence. From 1796 to 1798 Malleville was Governor of all three islands. He was also the first non-Lutheran to be governor. He was baptized in the Reformed Dutch Church and in 1773 applied for membership in the Moravian Church.

MARKOE, ABRAHAM, 1727-1806. A St. Cruzian who became prominent in the business and social life of Philadelphia as well as in the American Revolution. In 1774 he founded the first volunteer military association in what is now the United States--the Philadelphia Light Horse. He escorted General George Washington to New York. Markoe resigned his command in 1776 when Denmark proclaimed neutrality, since he was still a Danish citizen.

MARKOE, PETER, 1752-1792. Poet, dramatist and writer, son of Abraham Markoe. In 1790 he published one of the earliest comic operas written in America, "The Reconciliation." He also participated briefly in the American Revolution as a captain in his father's Philadelphia Light Horse militia.

MERWIN, JOHN DAVID, 1921- . Lawyer, politician, businessman and public official. He held the posts of Senator, 1955-1957; Government Secretary, 1957-1958; and Governor, 1958-1961.

MICHELSEN, H. A native of Schleswig, Denmark, who emigrated to St. Thomas in 1865. He became a successful merchant, famous for popularizing Virgin Islands bay rum toilet water.

MIKKELSEN, MIKKEL. Governor of St. Thomas in 1686. He was Harbor Master in Copenhagen in 1685 when sent out by the King as Commissioner to investigate Governor Milan's conduct. He jailed Milan and took him back to Denmark.

MILAN, GABRIEL, 1631-1689. He was named Governor of St. Thomas in 1684, partly because of his facility with languages. He turned out to be sickly and suspicious, and he whimsically played politics with the local planters, causing his rapid downfall. Milan was tried on charges of rebellion and was beheaded in Denmark in 1689.

MISS BLYDEN. A Christmas drink consisting of a spiced syrup mixed with rum and colored with prickly pear fruit.

MONETARY UNIT. Before 1904 the Virgin Islands had used the dollar system, with one V.I. dollar equal to 3.60 Danish kronen. Only coins were minted, the highest in value worth 20 cents(U. S.), while credit notes were used for paper money. In 1904 the franc became the monetary unit. One franc was worth 20-cents (U. S.) and was divided into 100 bits. Twenty-five- and 50-franc coins were minted in gold; those of lesser values were of silver or bronze. Today the dollar is again used.

MORAVIAN CHURCH. Officially organized in 1457 as "Unity of the Brethren, " the name Moravian was adopted since much of the group's early history centered in Moravia. After being reduced to remnants by the 1700's it was rebuilt largely due to the German Nobleman Count Zinzendorf, who sheltered its refugees in Saxony. There the church flourished and began a world-wide mission program. The first missionaries went to St. Thomas, arriving December 13, 1732. At present there are some eight Moravian Churches in the Virgin Islands. See also ZINZENDORF, COUNT NICOLAI.

MORAVIAN MISSIONARIES. German (Herrnhut) missionaries came to St. Thomas in 1732 to teach and Christianize the slaves. By 1835 their congregation included some 9508 slaves and only 960 free men.

MORON, ALONSO GRASEANO, 1909-1971. A distinguished educator and public official who held several important posts in the Islands. He is, however, especially noted as the first Negro President of Hampton Institute in Virginia.

MOTH, FRIEDRICK, ?-1746. The first governor of all three islands in the Danish West Indies, taking up these duties in 1736.

MOTH, FRIEDRICK, II, ?-1801. Captain, plantation owner on St. Croix and titular Councilor of State. He was named governor in 1770.

MUSIC. Despite numerous European countries having claimed the Virgin Islands, few traces exist of their influence in music. Rather, the West African influence has predominated. Contrary to popular belief, the calypso is a borrowed "folk-form" introduced in the 1930's. The music of the nearly extinct "scratch-bands" is authentically indigenous. Instruments used in this music originally consisted of African tom-toms, tambourines, bones, guiros, maracas, and 5-gallon kerosene cans. They were accompanied by "caruso" singers.

- N -

NAVAL GOVERNMENT. From their 1917 purchase and occupation by the U. S. until 1931, the Virgin Islands had a Naval government. A high-ranking naval officer served as governor and all principal positions were held by naval officers. The governor was appointed by the U. S. President, with the advice and consent of the Senate. Local laws and political institutions established by Denmark remained generally in force. In 1931 a civilian administration began, under the U. S. Department of Interior control. The 1936 Organic Act formalized civilian government. See also ORGANIC ACT OF 1936.

NAYGUR. A vulgar term for Negro.

NEMOURS, ALFRED, 1876-1943. A pianist and musical composer born in the Virgin Islands who gained some recognition in the German musical world, where he spent many years studying. Among his best known published works are "Song d'Amour," "Soirés de Berlin" and "Aire de Ballet."

NEW HERRNHUT [or New Hernhut]. A Moravian mission-compound established just east of Charlotte Amalie. It was an early center of the evangelistic movement. The name comes from the German town of Herrnhut in Oberlausitz, eastern Saxony.

NEWSPAPERS. Several newspapers have come and gone in the history of these islands. While nearly all have been in English, the earliest paper, the Royal Danish American Gazette, was bi-lingual. This paper began publishing on St. Croix in mid-1770. At the turn of the 18th Century the St. Croix Gazette appeared. Early 19th-Century papers included the Saint Thomas Gazette and Saint Tomas Tidende. The Tidende, in Danish, was a kind of official government gazette.

- O -

OBEAHISM [or Obiah.] Black magic, witchcraft. This was

prevalent in all social classes during the early period of West Indies colonization. However, Negroes convicted of its practice were severely punished.

OFFICIAL FLOWER. The yellow elder (or yellow cedar), Tecoma stans, was adopted by Governor Pearson's proclamation in June 1934. It is indigenous to all three of the islands and a constant bloomer.

OLDENDORP, C. G. A. An historian who accompanied the Moravian missionaries to the Danish West Indies; he published an early history of the islands in 1777.

ORGANIC ACT OF 1917. The First Organic Act, approved by the U. S. Congress March 3, 1917. It provided for a "temporary" government for the recently purchased Virgin Islands. It vested all military, civil and judicial authority in a governor and other persons whom the President might appoint to administrate until Congress should provide for a permanent government. All compatible Danish laws in effect at the time of transfer were to remain in force.

ORGANIC ACT OF 1936. Passed by Congress on June 22, 1936, this Act replaced the 1917 Act. This Act organized the Virgin Islands into an insular possession of two districts--the municipalities of St. Croix and St. Thomas, the latter including St. John. A separation of executive, legislative and judicial powers was provided. The Presidentially-appointed Governor could veto the legislature's actions. The post of Government Secretary (the second executive after the Governor) was also established. The U. S. Interior Secretary was directed to appoint an administrator for St. Croix, under provisions of this Act. The only elective offices established were those of the two municipal councils, which, meeting together, constituted the Legislative Assembly of the Virgin Islands.

ORGANIC ACT OF 1954. This Act was approved July 22, 1954. Innovations from the 1936 Organic Act included the establishment of nine executive departments and a unicameral legislative body of 11 senators, elected for two-year terms. The principal change provided by this Act however, was economic in nature. For every dollar of local revenue raised the federal government agreed to match it with one dollar, to be paid from revenues collected on rum shipped from the Virgin Islands to the U. S.

OTTLEY, EARLE H. A contemporary journalist, politician and labor leader.

OXHOLM, PETER LOTHARIUS, 1753-1827. Governor of St. Croix from 1815-1816. He went to the Danish West Indies in 1777 with orders to draw maps and diagrams, and make suggestions for defense in case the islands were exposed to attack.

- P -

PAIEWONSKY, RALPH, 1907- . Active in politics since 1936, he held several municipal and legislative posts before becoming Governor, 1961-1969. He is also noted for his extensive research in the 1930's with sea water fermentation, from which the rum distillation process that is the foundation of the Virgin Islands flourishing rum industry was developed.

PATOIS. The native Creole language is a mixture of languages, including Dutch, English and African dialects.

PEARSON, PAUL MARTIN, 1871-1938. He was the first civilian governor under U. S. sovereignty, holding the post from 1931 to 1935. He was the father of the noted American columnist Drew Pearson.

PEPE [or Peps]. Godfather.

PETROGRAPHS. These are stone writings made in pre-Columbian days and believed to be the work of Carib Indians. Several have been discovered in the Virgin Islands.

PIRACY. Piracy thrived in the West Indies in the 17th Century. It was one of the greatest handicaps to the early Danish colonists. St. Thomas gained a reputation as a resort for pirates, and probably would have been even more lenient except for the fear of reprisals from the British Navy. Among famed pirates in Virgin Islands history were Captain Kidd, Legendre and Tempest Roger. Piracy was not completely wiped out until 1825, when increased U. S. Navy patrols in the Caribbean finally ended the comparative free movement of pirate ships.

PISSARRO, CAMILLE, 1830-1903. He was born in St. Thomas, the son of a French Jewish merchant. Pissarro spent the last 50 years of his life in France, pursuing his desire to paint, and became one of the greatest painters in the world. By 1870 he was painting landscapes with the technique that would become known as Impressionism. His works are unique in this school. His Parisian scenes are considered the most successful revelations of light and atmosphere of the Impressionists.

PLESSEN, CHARLES ADOLPH VON. The Danish councilor who was instrumental in the purchase of St. Croix in 1733. He and Frederick Holmsted, Mayor of Copenhagen, were chiefly responsible for the successful negotiations and purchase from France for about $142, 000. Von Plessen convinced the stockholders and directors of the financially plagued Danish West India Company that purchasing St. Croix could rehabilitate the Company. Subsequently the Company reorganized and made a large investment in St. Croix.

POLITICAL PARTIES. Parties came into existence in 1937, after the 1936 Organic Act brought universal suffrage. In 1937 a group known as the Virgin Islands Progressive Guide was organized and put forth candidates. Previously, candidates ran as "independents." By 1940 the Guide swept the elections on a "Square Deal Ticket," patterned after Roosevelt's New Deal. It was the first formal political platform ever presented. This party originally existed only on St. Thomas. In 1942 it unsuccessfully tried to organize in St. Croix. In 1947 the Virgin Islands Liberal Party was founded, with one of its principal aims the popular election of the Governor. This party was in fact a rebel splinter group from the Progressive Guide. While both national U. S. parties, Republican and Democratic, have long had an organization in the Virgin Islands, only in recent years have they been prominent in local politics as well.

POPULATION see CENSUS

PROGRESSIVE GUIDE see POLITICAL PARTIES

PRO-SALE AND ANTI-SALE PARTIES. These two political groups were organized for and against the transfer of the Virgin Islands from Denmark to the U. S. They became active around 1900, especially on St. Croix. The Pro-Sale group was mainly estate owners, planters and sugar growers who sought the secure U. S. sugar market. Anti-Sale groups were mainly Danes or natives who were loyal to Denmark, or had economic advantages under the existing government.

PURCHASE AGREEMENT. The United States sought to purchase the Danish West Indies as early as 1865. The Civil War had served to create an interest in their military significance, since they had served as a refuge for ships during the North's blockade of southern ports. Denmark was also interested in a sale since by then the islands had lost their commercial value. A treaty of purchase in 1870 failed to gain Senate ratification. Several decades later, during the Spanish-American War, the Danish parliament rejected a new treaty proposal. The purchase was finally completed during World War I at a cost of $25 million, or $259 per acre. This made the purchase the most expensive territory ever purchased by the U. S.; it was also the smallest. The formal transfer of governmental powers occurred on March 31, 1917.

- R -

RAASLOFF, GENERAL WALDEMAR R. The Danish minister to the U. S. with whom Secretary of State Seward sought to negotiate a sale of the islands in 1865.

RALEIGH, SIR WALTER, 1552?-1618. This English navigator and colonist on an expedition to Virginia supposedly touched upon the island of St. Croix for a day.

RIISE, A. H., ?-1882. Danish millionaire who resided in the Virgin Islands and founded a company which still bears his name.

ROBERTS, LIONEL VALDEMAR, 1867-1946. A musician, journalist, legislator and athlete, he organized the Juvenile Band. He was Chairman of the Organic Act Commission of 1936.

ROHDE, LEWIN JURGEN. A harbor captain in St. Thomas who became the acting governor for about a month in 1830, when Governor Rosenhein fell off his horse and left the island for treatment.

ROTHSCHILD, FRANCIS. A native of St. Thomas, he was a pioneer of self-government for the Virgin Islands. As a militant liberal he fought for full rights of U. S. citizenship after the 1917 Organic Act was enacted.

- S -

ST. CROIX. The largest of the U. S. Virgin Islands with an area of 80 square miles and a 1970 population of 31, 779. Its early history was filled with European powers vying for control. From approximately 1597 when Sir Walter Raleigh is supposed to have touched here, the island remained unoccupied until about 1625. From then until 1649 the island was occupied by British, Dutch and even some French settlers from neighboring islands. While the English finally became supreme during this period, they were soon ousted by the Spaniards in 1650. Within months, however, a French force, led by the Knights of Malta defeated the Spanish garrison. From 1650 to 1733 St. Croix was entirely under the protection of France and the Knights of Malta. This was the age of Louis XIV, Colbert and Richelieu. St. Croix became Roman Catholic, while St. Thomas remained largely Lutheran, Dutch Reformed and Moravian. Under the French, St. Croix failed to develop. By 1695 the population numbered only 770, of which some 147 were whites. When it was sold to the Danes in 1733 it had become an abandoned, impoverished colony. St. Croix has always been the agricultural center of the islands.

ST. JOHN. The smallest of the three U. S. Virgin Islands, with an area of 20 square miles and a 1970 population of 1729. Two-thirds of the island is part of the Virgin Islands National Park, established by Congress in 1956. The Danish West India Company laid claim to St. John in 1684. It was 1717 before settlers from St. Thomas established a colony, however, since British hostility coming from neighboring Tortola hindered earlier colonization.

ST. THOMAS. Second largest of the U. S. Virgin Islands, with an area of 32 square miles and a 1970 population of 28, 960. It is some 14 miles long and has an average width of two miles. It was the island where the Danish colonization began and where commerce flourished. Most of the population lives in the capital of the Virgin Islands located here, Charlotte Amalie; as a result the two names "Charlotte Amalie" and "St. Thomas" are almost interchangeable. The port is considered the finest in the Caribbean and since colonial days it has been a thriving center of commerce.

SALT RIVER. On the island of St. Croix this is where Columbus is believed to have landed first in 1493.

SANTA ANA, ANTONIO LOPEZ, 1795?-1876. Four-time Mexican President renowned for his victory at the Alamo prior to Mexican-American War losses under his leadership. He lived in St. Thomas for a time, lavishing gold on carefree living. He popularized the use of Mexican silver dollars in the island's already unstable economy, which later nearly led to a riot in 1892 when banks refused to accept the Mexican currency.

SCHIMMELMANN, HEINRICH LUDWIG ERNST, 1743-1793. Governor General on St. Croix during the 1770's and 1780's.

SCHOLTEN, PETER CARL FREDERIK VON, 1784-1854. The dominant political and social figure in the Danish West Indies during the first half of the 19th Century. He was Governor of St. Thomas in 1823 and of all three islands after 1827. He arrived at the time of prosperity and led a fairly lavish nobleman's life. He was criticized for building an elaborate private home, which later became Government House. He was known for his compassion for the slaves and is credited with emancipating the slaves in 1848. He faced a series of charges and trials by his enemies from 1840 to 1847, largely due to the favor shown to Negro slaves. His proclamation of abolition was unpopular with the planters so he resigned and submitted himself to trial in Denmark. After lengthy proceedings and appeals he was acquitted of the charge of over-stepping his authority by the Danish Supreme Court on April 29, 1852.

SEAT OF GOVERNMENT. The first colonization effort in 1666 and the second in 1671 both placed the seat of government on St. Thomas. In 1748 it was moved to St. Croix where it remained until 1871. It was then returned to St. Thomas where it remains today.

SEWARD, WILLIAM HENRY, 1801-1872. U. S. Secretary of State under Lincoln who was anxious to purchase the Danish West Indies in the 1860's. He made a survey there in 1865 and offered Denmark $5 million for St. Thomas and St. John. St. Croix could not be included in the offer because the French had first claim by virtue of a 1733 treaty with Denmark. In 1867 a formal treaty was offered to Denmark, but it was pigeonholed by the Senate and died in April 1870. See also TREATY OF 1867.

SLAGELSE, KJELD JENSEN, ?-1672. A Danish Lutheran pastor who sailed with Erik Smidt in 1665 on the first Danish expedition to the West Indies. He established the first Lutheran congregation in 1666. When Governor Smidt died in June 1666, Slagelse became Acting Governor for a short time. He died on route to Denmark in 1672.

SLAVE REVOLTS. A serious revolt on St. John began in November 1733. It was attributed to hard measures taken by the governor to stop slaves from escaping to neighboring islands. In this revolt the blacks held nearly all of St. John for nearly six months, and 42 of 98 plantations were destroyed or damaged. A slave rebellion threatened St. Croix in 1746 but was quickly put down. More serious outbreaks occurred here in December 1759. For the revolt of 1848 see the following entry.

SLAVERY. The importation of slaves to work the sugar plantations began as early as the late 1600's, but the total slave population reached only some 30, 000. The islands were mainly used as a distribution center for sending slaves to other points, rather than as a place of employment of great numbers. Negroes clearly outnumbered whites at the time of their emancipation in 1848. After this, an almost universal decline in the economy began. Previously, in 1804, Denmark had become the first country in the world to prohibit the importation of slaves. In 1847 slavery was abolished by a Danish decree that was to take effect over a 12-year transition period. A revolt by the slaves in 1848 caused the islands' Governor von Scholten (which see) to eliminate this transition period and put the decree immediately into effect.

SMIDT [also Smed], ERIK NIELSEN, ?-1666. The first actual Governor of the Danish West Indies, by Royal appointment of June 8, 1665. He captained the first voyage from Denmark to the West Indies. On March 30, 1666 he took possession of St. Thomas in the name of the Danish King. He died only three months later and the colony soon failed.

STIVER BUSH. A plant whose small rounded leaves resembled an obsolete Danish coin called a "Styve."

SUGAR. The rapid growth in economic importance of sugar cane began in the 18th Century. St. Croix is the main producer as it was in the past. Production there reached 25 million pounds in the 1780's. The all-time high in production was in 1812: 46 million pounds.

- T -

TANIA. A tropical rootcrop, tasting like a potato. The large elephant-eared leaf contrasts to the potato vine, however. It is a favorite crop of the Chacha farmers. See also CHACHAS.

TAYLOR, CHARLES E., 1843-?. An Englishman of varied careers who travelled throughout the American continent. Because of a critical illness he stopped in St. Croix, later making it his home. He was an author, violinist, painter and engineer, but took up medicine late in life. He fought against the closed entrance to the medical profession and was a partisan of the new homeopathy system, of preventive medicine, and of the use of hypnosis and electrical treatments (while opposing vaccination). He gained fame for successfully treating "incurable cases." But the medical monopoly brought him to task for practicing without a license. The populace paid his fines and gave him money to complete his medical studies in the U. S.

THORMOHLEN, GEORGE. A venturesome Bergen merchant to whom the Danish West India Company leased the entire island of St. Thomas in 1690, for a ten-year period. Until then the shareholders had not received any dividend from the Company and it sought to recover financially. He also had to provide a small garrison for the colony. The Company took over again in 1694 before the lease ran out.

TOBACCO. It was grown in the Virgin Islands from earliest colonial times, but declined rapidly and was replaced by sugar.

TODMAN, TERRANCE, 1926- . St. Thomas-born, he currently (1972) serves as U. S. Ambassador to the Republic of Chad. A political science specialist, he has made his career in the State Department.

TRANSFER DAY. Annual official holiday in the Virgin Islands. Celebrated March 31st, the day in 1917 when the islands were formally transferred to U. S. authority.

TRANSFER TREATY OF 1916. This was the treaty whereby the Danish West Indies were purchased by the United States. It was signed on August 4, 1916; its ratification was proclaimed on January 25, 1917. The civil rights and political status of the inhabitants come under the determination of the U. S. Congress by this treaty. The purchase price for the three islands was $25 million in gold coin. See also PURCHASE AGREEMENT.

TREATY OF AMIENS. A treaty of February 22, 1802, between Denmark and Great Britain. It restored the islands to Denmark, which had lost them to the British fleet under Admiral Duckworth and General Tregg in April 1801.

TREATY OF 1867. First treaty negotiated between U. S. and Denmark for purchase of Danish West Indies, it followed two years of negotiations led by Secretary of State Seward of the U. S. Two principal terms of the treaty were: only the islands of St. John and St. Thomas were included, and a plebiscite on the sale was to be held on the islands. Despite Danish parliament upper house (Landsting) approval in January 1868, and after overwhelming support for the sale shown by the plebiscite, U. S. Senate rejected action on the treaty since it was in the middle of impeachment proceedings against President Johnson. In the subsequent election of 1868, Grant was elected President; he was not in favor of the purchase. Official U. S. rejection of the 1867 proposed treaty came in 1870. The sale price for St. Thomas and St. John was to have been $7. 5 million.

TREATY OF 1902. A second treaty of sale was negotiated between Denmark and U. S., this time for all three islands of the Danish West Indies. It failed by two votes to win approval in the Danish Parliament. The U. S. had offered $5 million for the three--St. John, St. Thomas, and St. Croix. U. S. purchase was motivated now by the fear that an unfriendly European power might obtain the islands. Evidence is lacking for a rumor published at the time that pressure from Germany prevented Denmark's approval. Following the rejection, a Royal Commission was sent from Denmark to study measures for economic, social and administrative improvements. It recommended creation of a Virgin Islands representative to the Danish Parliament.

"TRIANGLE TRADE." A three-cornered slave trade, between Boston, North Africa, and the Danish West Indies. Sugar made into molasses in the islands was then shipped to New England and distilled into rum; from there the rum was shipped to Africa to trade for slaves, who were brought to the islands to harvest more sugar. Outgrowths of this trade were New England sailing ship development and Boston rum distilleries some of which are still in operation.

- V -

VIRGIN ISLANDS. Columbus discovered the islands in 1493 and named them after the Virgin of St. Ursula, the sailors' patron saint; supposedly the numerous islets jutting into the sea reminded him of nuns kneeling in prayer.

VIRGIN ISLANDS CORPORATION. In 1934 the U. S. Government created the Virgin Islands Company as a relief and rehabilitation project for the island of St. Croix. On June 30, 1949, this company was succeeded by the Virgin Islands Corporation (VICORP), with broader economic development objectives.

VIRGIN ISLANDS NATIONAL PARK. Established in 1956 on St. John Island by Act of U. S. Congress, it covers a majority of the island's 12, 000 acres. The park was made possible through a contribution of some 5000 acres of land by the Rockefeller family. It is administrated by the U. S. National Park Service and is the only U. S. National Park in the Caribbean.

- W -

WALTERSDORFF, ERNST FREDERICK, 1755-1820. A late 18th-Century Governor General of St. Croix, he also held several other diplomatic and military posts, including Danish Ambassador to Paris in 1803. He was admitted into the nobility in 1819.

WESTEND. Creole name for the town of Frederiksted, St. Croix.

WICHARO. A grooved gourd used as a musical instrument. Probably taken from the Spanish "Guicharo."

- Y -

YELLOW BREAST BIRD. The official bird of the Virgin Islands. Also called the "Sugar Bird."

YULEE, DAVID LEVY, 1810-1886. Prominent Florida lawyer, politician and legislator at the time of American Civil War. Born in St. Thomas of a Portuguese father, Yulee went to Florida as a boy to study. There he remained. In the 1840's he was a U. S. Representative and then a Senator from Florida. He advocated secession from the Union in 1850 and was later a member of the Confederate Congress. Imprisoned for a time after the war, he was released by General Grant.

- Z -

ZINZENDORF, COUNT NICOLAI LOUIS VON. German nobleman and prominent Moravian missionary who settled in the Danish West Indies in the 18th Century. In Saxony he had saved the early church from destruction by giving refuge to its followers in 1732. See also MORAVIAN CHURCH.

BIBLIOGRAPHY

General Caribbean

Albanell, Norah. et al. Cuba, Dominican Republic, Haiti and Puerto Rico; A Selected Bibliography. Gainesville: University of Florida, School for Inter-American Studies, 1956.

Alfredo, Antonio. The Geographical and Historical Dictionary of America and the West Indies. 5 vols. London, 1812-1815.

Arciniegas, Germán. Caribbean Sea of the New World. New York: New World, 1946.

Bayitch, S. A. Latin America and the Caribbean, A Bibliographical Guide to Works in English. Coral Gables, Fla: University of Miami Press, 1967.

Comitas, Lambros. Caribbean 1900-1965: A Topical Bibliography. Seattle: University of Washington Press, 1968.

Crocker, John. The Centaur Guide to Bermuda, the Bahamas, Hispaniola, Puerto Rico and the Virgin Islands. Fontwell: Centaur, 1968.

Curtain, Philip D. The Atlantic Slave Trade, A Census. Madison: University of Wisconsin Press, 1969.

Fiske, Amon Kidder. The West Indies, a History of the Islands of the West Indian Archipelago. New York, 1906.

Fox, Annette B. Freedom and Welfare in the Caribbean; a Colonial Dilemma. New York, 1949.

Hamm, Margarita A. America's New Possessions and Spheres of Influence. London, 1899.

Harlow, Vincent T. Colonizing Expeditions to the West Indies and Guiana, 1623-1667. London, 1925.

Lewis, Gordon K. The Growth of the Modern West Indies. New York: Monthly Review Press, 1968.

Mims, Stewart L. Colbert's West India Policy. New Haven: Yale University Press, 1912.

Netherlands Universities Foundation for International Cooperation. Developments Toward Self-Government in the Caribbean. A Symposium. The Hague: W. VanHoeve Ltd., 1955.

Newton, Arthur Percival. The European Nations in the West Indies, 1493-1688. London: A & C Black, 1933.

Preiswerk, Roy. Documents on International Relations in the Caribbean. Caribbean Documents No. 1, Institute of Caribbean Studies, University of Puerto Rico, Rio Piedras, 1970.

Proudfoot, Mary. Britain and the United States in the Caribbean. New York: Praeger, 1954.

Raynal, Guillaume T. F. A Philosophical and Political History of the Settlements and Trade of the Europeans in the East and West Indies. Edinburgh, 1762.

Waugh, Alex. The Sugar Islands. London: Cassell & Co., 1958.

Wilgus, A. Curtis, ed. The Caribbean at Mid-Century. Gainesville: University of Florida Press, 1951.

________. Histories and Historians of Hispanic America. 3rd ed. New York: Cooper Square, 1965.

Williams, Eric. Capitalism and Slavery. Chapel Hill: University of North Carolina Press, 1944.

BIBLIOGRAPHY

Puerto Rico

Aitken, Thomas. Poet in the Fortress: the Story of Luis Muñoz Marín. New York: New American Library, 1964.

Alegría, José S. Cincuenta años de literatura puertorriqueña. San Juan: Academia Puertorriqueña de la Lengua, 1955.

Alegría, Ricardo. "The Archaic Tradition in Puerto Rico," American Antiquity, 21 (1955).

________. Descubrimiento, conquista y colonización de Puerto Rico, 1493-1599. San Juan: Colección de Estudios Puertorriqueños, 1969.

Almanaque Puertorriqueño Asenjo. San Juan: Tipografía San Juan, n. d.

American Academy of Political and Social Science. The Annals. Puerto Rico: A Study in Democratic Development. Philadelphia, 1953.

Anderson, Robert W. Party Politics in Puerto Rico. Stanford, Calif.: Stanford University Press, 1965.

Angelis, Pedro de. Miscelaneas puertorriqueñas. Colección de artículos históricos biográficos. San Juan: Tipografía de Terreras, 1894.

Arana Soto, Salvador. Defensa de los capitanes generales españoles con una nueva interpretación del siglo XIX puertorriqueño. San Juan: Tipografía Maguza, 1968.

________. Historia de nuestra calamidades. San Juan: Tipografía Maguza, 1968.

Babín, María Teresa. La cultura de Puerto Rico. San Juan: Instituto de Cultura Puertorriqueña, 1970.

Barbosa de Rosario, Pilar. De Baldorioty a Barbosa. San Juan: Imprenta Venezuela, 1957.

Barbusse, E. The United States in Puerto Rico, 1898-1900. Chapel Hill: University of North Carolina Press, 1966.

Benton, Elbert J. International Law and Diplomacy of the Spanish-American War. Baltimore, 1908.

Berga y Ponce de León, Pablo. Vida histórica del Tribunal Supremo. San Juan: Tipografía Real Hermanos, 1939.

Blanco, Tomás. "Anglocomodismos en el vernacular puertorriqueño." Revista del Instituto de Cultura Puertorriqueño, XIII, Num. 36 (enero-marzo, 1970), pp. 22-26.

_______. Pronturario histórico de Puerto Rico. 2d ed. San Juan: Editorial Biblioteca de Autores Puertorriqueños, 1943.

Bothwell, Reece B., y Cruz Monclova, Lidio. Los documentos: que dicen? Río Piedras: Editorial Universitaria, 1962.

Brau, M. M. Island in the Crossroads, the History of Puerto Rico. New York: Doubleday, Zenith Books, 1968.

Brau, Salvador. La colonización de Puerto Rico. San Juan: Heraldo Español, 1907.

_______. Historia de Puerto Rico. New York: D. Appleton & Co., 1904.

Cadilla de Martínez, María. Costumbres y tradiciones de mi tierra. San Juan: Imprenta Venezuela, 1938.

Callejo Ferrer, Fernando. Música y músicos puertorriqueños. Tipografía Cantero Fernández y Cia. 1915.

Canet, Dalmau. Luis Muñoz Rivera. San Juan: Imprenta El Boletín Mercantil, 1917.

Caplow, Theodore. The Urban Ambience: a Study of San Juan. Río Piedras, 1964.

Caro Costas, Aida Raquel. Ramón Power y Geralt. San Juan, 1969.

Carreras, Carlos N. Hombres y mujeres de Puerto Rico. México: Editorial Orión, 1957.

Carreras, Juan. Santiago Iglesias Patín, su vida, su obra, su pensamiento. San Juan: Editorial Club de la Prensa, 1967.

Carroll, H. K. Report on the Island of Porto Rico. Washington, 1899.

Coll y Toste, Cayetano. Boletín histórico de Puerto Rico. San Juan, 1914-1926.

_______. Historia de la esclavitud en Puerto Rico. San Juan: Sociedad de Autores Puertorriqueños, 1969.

_______. Prehistoria de Puerto Rico. San Juan: Imprenta el Boletín Mercantil, 1907.

_______. Puertorriqueños ilustres. 2d Selección. Bilbao: Editorial Vasco Americano, n. d.

Córdova, Pedro Tomás de. Memorias geográficas, históricas, económicas y estadísticas de la isla de Puerto Rico. 2d ed. San Juan: Instituto de Cultura Puertorriqueña, 1968.

Corkran, Herbert Jr. From Formal to Informal International Cooperation in the Caribbean. (Arnold Foundation Monographs, XVII.) Dallas: Southeran Methodis University, 1966.

Cruz Colón, José Antonio. Bibliografía sobre literatura de administración pública relacionada con Puerto Rico (1898-1968). Río Piedras, 1969.

Cruz Monclova, Lidio. Historia del año "87". Río Piedras: Editorial Universitaria, 1958.

Degetau y Gonzales, Federico. The Political Status of Porto Rico. Washington, 1902.

DeGranda, Germán. Transculturacíon e interferencia lingüística en el Puerto Rico contemporáneo. Bogota: Instituto Caro y Cuervo, 1968.

Díaz Soler, Luis M. Historia de la esclavitud negra en

Puerto Rico, 1493-1890. Rio Piedras: Univ. of Puerto Rico, 1953.

Dossick, John Jesse. Doctoral Research on Puerto Rico and Puerto Ricans. New York: New York University, 1967.

Enamorado Cuesta, José. Porto Rico: Past and Present. New York: Eureka Printing Co., 1929.

Epstein, Erwin H., ed. Politics and Education in Puerto Rico: A Documentary Survey of the Language Issue. Metuchen, N.J.: Scarecrow Press, 1970.

Estado Libre Asociado de Puerto Rico. Junta Estatal de Elecciones. Leyes de Puerto Rico anotadas. Oxford, N.H.: Equity Publishing Co., 1968.

________. Junta de Planificación. Indicadores socio-económicos por regiones. Septiembre, 1970.

Esteves Volkers, Luis. Tarjetero histórico. Madrid: Gráficas R. Manzanas, 1960.

Farr, Kenneth R. The Problem of Institutionalization of a Political Party: The Case of the Partido Popular Democrático of Puerto Rico. Ph.D. Dissertation, Tulane University, 1971. (Forthcoming publication by Inter American University Press, San Juan.)

________. Puerto Rico Election Factbook, November 5, 1968. Washington, D.C.: Institute for the Comparative Study of Political Systems, 1968.

Fawkes, J. W. The Aborigenes of Puerto Rico and Neighboring Islands. Washington, 1907.

Fernández Juncos, Manuel. Antología puertorriqueña. New York: Editores Hinds, Hayden and Eldrege, 1944.

________. Semblanzas puertorriqueñas. Puerto Rico, Tipografía de J. Gonzales Front, 1888.

Fernández Méndez, Eugenio. ed. Crónicas de Puerto Rico, Volumen I (1493-1797). San Juan: Ediciones del Gobierno Estado Libro Asociado de Puerto Rico, 1957.

________. Desarrollo histórico de la sociedad puertorriqueño. San Juan: Instituto de Cultura Puertorriqueña, 1959.

_______. Historia cultural de Puerto Rico, 1493-1968. San Juan: Ediciones El Cemi, 1970.

_______. The Sources of Puerto Rican Culture History. San Juan: Ediciones El Cemi, 1967.

Figueroa, Loida. Breve historia de Puerto Rico. Río Piedras: Editorial Edil, 1968.

Fitzpatrick, Joseph F. Puerto Rican Americans. Englewood Cliffs, N. J.: Prentice-Hall, 1971.

Flinter, George Dawson. An Account of the Present State of the Island of Puerto Rico. (New impression of 1834 ed.). London: Frank Cass and Co., n. d.

Fonfrías Rivera, Ernesto Juan. De la lengua de Isabela la católica a la taina del cacique Agueybana. San Juan: Editorial Club de la Prensa, 1969.

García Passalacqua, Juan M. La crisis política en Puerto Rico (1962-1966). San Juan: Ediciones Edil, 1970.

Gautier Dapena, Jose A. Trayectoria de pensamiento liberal puertorriqueño en el siglo XIX. San Juan: Instituto de Cultura, 1963.

Gaztambide y Arán, Francisco. La isla de Puerto Rico. New York: Rand McNally, 1941.

Gonzales Ginorio, José. El descubrimiento de Puerto Rico. San Juan: Imprenta Venezuela, 1936.

Goodsell, Charles T. Administration of a Revolution. Cambridge: Harvard University Press, 1965.

Gotas históricas de Puerto Rico. San Juan: Fleishman Puerto Rico, 1971.

Gualberto Gómez, Juan, y Sandías y Burín, Antonio. La isla de Puerto Rico. Madrid: Jose Gil y Navarro, 1891.

Hanson, Earl Parker. Transformation: The Story of Modern Puerto Rico. New York: Simon & Schuster, 1955.

Hernández Aquino, Luis. Diccionario de voces indígenas de Puerto Rico. Bilbao: Editorial Vasco Americana, 1969.

Hibbes, Thomas and Picó, Rafael. ed. Industrial Development of Puerto Rico and the Virgin Islands. Port of Spain, Caribbean Commission, 1948.

Hostos, Adolfo de. Historia de San Juan, ciudad murada: 1521-1898. San Juan: Instituto de Cultura Puertorriqueña, 1966.

_______. Tesauro de datos históricos. 3 Vol. San Juan: Imprenta del Gobierno de Puerto Rico, 1948, 1949, 1951.

Hostos y Bonilla, Eugenio María de. Obras completas. 2d ed. San Juan: Instituto de Cultura Puertorriqueña, 1969.

Hunt, William W. The Book of Governors, 1509-1935. Los Angeles: Washington Tipographers, 1935.

Hunter, Robert J. The Historical Evolution of the Relationship between the United States and Puerto Rico: 1898-1963. Ph. D. dissertation. University of Pittsburgh, 1963.

Infiesta, Alejandro. La exposición de Puerto Rico. San Juan: Imprenta El Boletín Mercantil, 1895.

Instituto de Cultura Puertorriqueña. Guía al Archivo General de Puerto Rico. San Juan: Archivo General de Puerto Rico, 1964.

Ireland, G. "Spanish Audiencia in Puerto Rico," Tulane Law Review, 20 (1945).

Ledru, Andres Pierre. Viaje a la Isla de Puerto Rico. Traducción de Julio L. y de Vizcarrondo. Puerto Rico: Imprenta Militar de J. Gonzales, 1863.

Lewis, Gordon K. "Puerto Rico: Case Study of Change in an Underdeveloped Area," Journal of Politics, 18:4 (Nov. 1955), 614-650.

_______. Puerto Rico: Freedom and Power in the Caribbean. New York: Monthly Review Press, 1963.

El Libro de Puerto Rico. San Juan: Editorial El Imparcial,

annually.

Limon de Arce, José. Arecibo Histórico. Manati, Puerto Rico: Editorial Angel Rosado, 1938.

Llorens, Washington. El Habla Popular de Puerto Rico. Rio Piedras: Editorial Edil, 1971.

Lugo-Silva, Enrique. The Tugwell Administration in Puerto Rico, 1941-1946. San Juan: Editorial Cultura, 1955.

Malaret, Augusto. Vocabulario de Puerto Rico. San Juan: Imprenta Venezuela, 1937.

Maldonado, Teofilo. Hombres de primera plana. San Juan: Editorial Campos, 1958.

Maldonado-Denis, Manuel. Puerto Rico: una interpretación historico-social. Mexico: Siglo XXI Editores, 1969.

Massa, Gaetano y Vivas, José Luis. History of Puerto Rico. New York: Las Americas, 1969.

Mathews, Thomas. General Survey of the material related to Puerto Rico held by the Library of Congress. Washington: Hispanic Foundation, 1956.

________. Puerto Rican Politics and the New Deal. Gainesville: University of Florida Press, 1960.

________ and Andic, Font. editors. Politics and Economics in the Caribbean. 2d ed. rev. Rio Piedras: Institute of Caribbean Studies, University of Puerto Rico, 1970.

Menéndez de Valdés, Diego. Descripción de la isla y la fortificación que se hace y la artillería. Carta al Presidente del Real Consejo de las Indias, 1587. Archivo General de las Indias.

Miller, Paul G. Historia de Puerto Rico. Chicago: Rand McNally, 1922.

Mintz, Sidney W. "The Culture History of a Puerto Rico Sugar Cane Plantation, 1876-1949," Hispanic American Historical Review, 33:2 (May 1953), p224-251.

Mixer, K. Porto Rico: History and Conditions. New York, 1926.

Montalvo Guenard, J. L. Rectificaciones históricas (El Descubrimiento de Boriquén). Ponce: Editorial del Llano, 1933.

Morales Cabrera, P. Puerto Rico indígena. San Juan: Imprenta Venezuela, 1932.

Morales Carrión, Arturo. "The Historical Roots and Political Significance of Puerto Rico," in: The Caribbean: British, Dutch, French, United States, ed. by A. Curtis Wilgus. Gainesville: University of Florida Press, 1958.

________. Puerto Rico and the Non-Hispanic Caribbean. 2d ed. Rio Piedras: University of Puerto Rico, 1971.

Morse, Richard M. "The Deceptive Transformation of Puerto Rico." Paper delivered at the Conference on Social Science Historical Study, University of Michigan, May 1959.

Muñoz Marín, Luis. Historia del Partido Popular Democrático. San Juan: Editorial Caribe, 1952.

Muñoz Morales, Luis. El status político de Puerto Rico. San Juan: Tipografía El Compás, 1921.

Murga Sanz, Vicente. compilador. Historia documental de Puerto Rico. 3 Vol. Río Piedras: Universidad de Puerto Rico.

"Natalicios de puertorriqueños ilustres," Isla, 2:3-4 (dic., 1970-enero, 1971).

Negrón Muñoz, Angela. Mujeres de Puerto Rico; desde el período de colonización hasta el primer tercio del siglo XX. San Juan: Imprenta Venezuela, 1935.

Neumann Gandia, Eduardo. Benefactores y hombres notables de Puerto Rico. 2 Vol. Ponce, 1896, 1899.

New York Academy of Science. Scientific Survey of Porto Rico and the Virgin Islands. New York: The Academy, 1919.

Nieves Falcón, Luis. Diagnóstico de Puerto Rico. Río Piedras: Editorial Edil, 1972.

Osuna, J. J. A History of Puerto Rico. Río Piedras, 1949.

Oviedo, González Fernández de. Historia general y natural de las indias. 19 tomos. Madrid, 1535.

Pabon, Milton, Anderson, Robert y Rivera, Victor. Los derechos y los partidos políticos en la sociedad puertorriqueña. San Juan: Ediciones Edil, 1968.

Pagán, Bolívar. Historia de los partidos políticos puertorriqueños. 2 tomos. San Juan: Librería Campos, 1959.

Pedreira, Antonio S. Bibliografía puertorriqueña, 1493-1930. Madrid, 1932.

_______. Insularismo. Madrid: Tipografía Artística, 1934.

Perea, Juan Augusto y Perea, Salvador. Historia del adelantado Juan Ponce de León. Caracas: Tipografía Cosmos, 1929.

Pérez de Bueso, Blanca. Leyendas indias del viento. San Juan: Editorial del Departamiento de Instrucción Publica, 1967.

Pérez Marchand, Monelisa. Historia de las ideas en Puerto Rico. San Juan: Instituto de Cultura Puertorriqueño, 1960.

Picó, Rafael. Geografía de Puerto Rico. 2 parts. Río Piedras: Editorial Universitaria.

Puerto Rico. Municipio de San Juan. Actas del cabildo de San Juan Bautista de Puerto Rico, 1803-1809. España: M. Pareja, 1970.

Puerto Rico. Office of the Commonwealth in Washington. Documents on the Constitutional History of Puerto Rico. Washington: Hennage Lithograph Co., 1964.

Puerto Rico. Reconstruction Administration. Puerto Rico, A Guide to the Island of Boriquén. New York: The University Society, 1940.

Quién es quién en Puerto Rico? San Juan: Real Hermanos, Inc., 1933.

Quiñones, Francisco Mariano. _Apuntes para la historia de Puerto Rico._ Mayagüez: Tipografía Comercial, 1888.

______. _Historia de los partidos reformista y conservador._ Mayagüez: Tipografía Comercial, 1889.

Ramírez Brau, Enrique. _Cofresí, historia y geneología de un Pirata._ San Juan: Casa Baldrich, 1945.

Ramírez de Arellano, Rafael. _Los huracanes de Puerto Rico._ Río Piedras: Universidad de Puerto Rico, 1932.

Ramos de Santiago, Carmen. _El gobierno de Puerto Rico._ Río Piedras: Editorial Universitaria, 1970.

Reck, D. _Puerto Rico and the Virgin Islands._ New York, 1939.

Rivera de Alvarez, Josefina. _Diccionario de literatura puertorriqueña._ Río Piedras: Ediciones de la Torre, Universidad de Puerto Rico, 1955.

Rivero, Angel. _Crónica de la guerra hispano-americana en Puerto Rico._ Madrid: Sucesores de Rivadeneyra, 1922.

Rives Tovar, Federico. _Enciclopedia Puertorriqueña Ilustrada._ 3 tomos. New York: Plus Ultra Educational Publishing, 1970.

Rosario, Rubén del. _Vocabulario puertorriqueño._ Sharon, Conn: The Troutman Press, 1965.

Rowe, L. S. _The United States and Porto Rico._ New York: Longmans, Green and Co., 1904.

Sandis, Eva E. _The Puerto Rican Experience._ New York: Simon and Schuster, Inc., 1970.

Santana, Arturo F. _The United States and Puerto Rico._ Ph. D. dissertation. University of Chicago, 1954.

Senior, Clarence. _Strangers then Neighbors: from Pilgrims to Puerto Ricans._ New York, 1961.

Stahl, Agustín. Fundación de Aguadilla. San Juan: Tipografía Boletín Mercantil, 1910.

Sterling, Philip and Brau, María. The Quiet Rebels: four Puerto Rican Leaders: José Celso Barbosa, Luis Muñoz Rivera, José De Diego and Luis Muñoz Marin. N.Y. Doubleday. 1968.

Tapia y Rivera, Alejandro. Biblioteca historica de Puerto Rico. San Juan: Instituto de Literatura Puertorriqueña, 1945.

________. Mis memorias a Puerto Rico como lo encontré y como lo dejo. New York: DeLaisne and Rossboro, 1928.

Todd, Roberto H. Desfile de gobernadores de Puerto Rico, 1898-1943. 2d ed. Madrid: Ediciones Ibero-Americanas, 1966.

Torres Asensio, Joaquín. Fuentes históricos sobre Colón y América. 4 Vol. Madrid: S. E. de San Francisco de Salas, 1892.

Tugwell, Rexford G. The Stricken Land; the Story of Puerto Rico. Garden City, N. Y., 1947.

Ubeda y Delgado, Manuel. Isla de Puerto Rico. San Juan: Tipografía del Boletín Mercantil, 1878.

United States-Puerto Rico Commission on the Status of Puerto Rico. Status of Puerto Rico. Washington: U. S. Government Printing Office, 1966.

The U. S. Overseas: Puerto Rico, Territories. New York: Time-Life Books, 1969.

Van Middeldyk, R. A. The History of Puerto Rico from the Spanish Discovery to the American Occupation. New York, 1903.

Velásquez, Gonzalo. compilador. Anuario bibliográfico puertorriqueño. Río Piedras: Biblioteca de la Universidad, 1950.

Wagenheim, Kal. Puerto Rico, a Profile. New York: Praeger Publishing Co., 1970.

Wells, Henry. "Ideology and Leadership in Puerto Rican Politics." American Political Science Review, 49:1 (Jan. 1955), 22-39.

________. The Modernization of Puerto Rico. Cambridge: Harvard University Press, 1969.

Wilgus, A. Curtis, ed. The Caribbean: Its Hemispheric Significance. Gainesville: University of Florida Press, 1967.

BIBLIOGRAPHY

U. S. Virgin Islands

Alexander, Joseph. The Story of Transfer. n. p., 1942.

Anderson, Lillian S. Up and Down the Virgin Islands. Oxford, N. H.: Equity Pub. Co., 1963.

Baa, Enid M., compiler. Theses on Caribbean Topics, 1778-1968. (Caribbean Bibliographic Series No. 1.) Río Piedras: Institute of Caribbean Studies, University of Puerto Rico Press, 1970.

Babcock, C. E. "Danish West Indies: A List of English References," Library Journal, 42, (1917) 422-423.

Bigelow, Poultney. The Children of the Nations: A Study of Colonization and its Problems. New York: McClure Philips, 1901.

Booy, Theodor H. de, and Paris, John T. The Virgin Islands, Our New Possessions and the British Islands. Philadelphia: J. B. Lippincott, 1918.

Bough, James A., and Macridis, Roy C., editors. Virgin Islands, America's Caribbean Outpost. Wakefield, Mass., Williams Pub. Co., 1970.

Brock, H. G. The Danish West Indies: their Resources and Commercial Importance. Washington, D. C.: G. P. O., 1917.

Brown, Boyd J. Report on the Virgin Islands Company. Christiansted, 1941.

Bullen, Ripley P. "The Preceramic Krum Bay Site, Virgin Islands and its Relationship to the Peopling of the Caribbean." Internationalen Amerikanstenkongresse, 1902, p398-403.

Campbell, Albert A. "St. Thomas Negroes--a Study of Personality and Culture," Psychological Monographs, 1943.

Canegata, D. C. St. Croix at the 20th Century. New York: Carlton Press, 1968.

Christensen, Carlo. Peter von Scholten; A Chapter of the History of the Virgin Islands. Lemvih, Denmark: G. Nielsens, 1955.

Cochran, Hamilton. These are the Virgin Islands. New York: Prentice-Hall, 1937.

Conover, Helen F., compiler. The Virgin Islands of the United States; a List of References, 1922-1936. Washington: Government Printing Office, 1937.

Creque, Darwin D. The U. S. Virgin Islands and the Eastern Caribbean. Philadelphia: Whitmore Pub. Co., 1968.

The Daily News. Special 40th Anniversary Edition. St. Thomas, August 1, 1970.

Danish West Indian Society. The Danish West Indies in Old Pictures. n. p., 1967.

Denmark. Royal Danish Academy of Fine Arts. Department of Town Planning. Three Towns, Conservation and Renewal of Charlotte Amalie, Christiansted and Frederiksted. Copenhagen: Tutein and Koch, 1965.

Desmond, R. W. "Caribbean Laboratory, U. S. A." Current History, 46 (1937).

Egan, Maurice Francis. Recollections of a Happy Life. New York, n. p., 1924.

Eggleston, George T. The Virgin Islands. Princeton: Van Nostrand Co., 1959.

Evans, Luther H. The Virgin Islands: From Naval Base to New Deal. Ann Arbor: J. W. Edwards, 1945.

Evans, Waldo. The Virgin Islands of the U. S.; a General Report by the Governor. Washington, D. C.: G. P. O., 1928.

Friends of Denmark Society. 50 Years. Special Publication Commemorating the 50th Anniversary of Virgin Islands transfer to the U. S. St. Thomas, 1967.

Gosnèr, Pamela. Historic Architecture of the U. S. Virgin Islands. Durham: Moore Pub. Co., 1971.

Gould, Lyman J. Raices de la política colonial de los Estados Unidos. Rio Piedras: Universidad de Puerto Rico, 1969.

Griffin, A. P. C. A List of Books on the Danish West Indies. Washington, D. C.: G. P. O., 1901.

Gutiérrez de Arce, Manuel. La colonización danesa en las islas vírgenes. Sevilla, Escuela de Estudios Hispan-americanos de la Universidad de Sevilla, 1945.

Haas, W. H., ed. The American Empire: A Study of the Outlying Territories of the United States. Chicago, 1940.

Hannau, Hans W. The Virgin Islands: St. Thomas, St. Croix, St. John. Garden City, N. Y.: Doubleday, 1965.

Harrigan, Norwell and Varlack, Pearl. The British Virgin Islands, a Chronology. Tortola, British Virgin Islands: Research and Consulting Services Ltd., 1970.

Heckert, Eleanor Louise. Muscovado. Garden City, N. Y.: Doubleday, 1968.

Henle, Fritz. Virgin Islands. New York: Hastings House, 1949.

Hesselberg, E. "Account of the Negro Rebellion on St. Croix," Journal of Negro History, 40 (1926).

Hill, Valdemar. A Golden Jubilee: Virgin Islanders on the Go Under the American Flag. New York: Carlton Press, 1967.

Holbrook, Sabra. The American West Indies, Puerto Rico and the Virgin Islands. New York, N. Y.: Meredith Press, 1969.

Hoover, Donald D. "The Virgin Islands Under American Rule." Foreign Affairs, 4:4(1925-26), 503-506.

Horlyk, Lucie. In Danish Times. St. Thomas, 1969.

Hutton, Joseph Edward. A History of the Moravian Missions. London, Moravian Church, n. d.

Jarvis, José Antonio. Brief History of the Virgin Islands. St. Thomas: The Art Shop, 1938.

________. The Virgins and Their People. Philadelphia: Dorrance and Co., 1944.

Jennings, J. E. Our American Tropics. New York, 1938.

Kay, Ernest, ed. Dictionary of Caribbean Biography. London: Melrose Press, 1970.

Keller, Albert. "Notes on the Danish West Indies," Annals of the American Academy of Political and Social Science, 22 (1902), 97-110.

King, Lis, ed. St. Thomas Directory. St. Thomas: Island Profiles, 1962.

Knox, John P. Knox Original History of the Danish West Indies, 1688-1848. New York: Adolph Sixto, 1922.

Knud-Hansen, Knud. From Denmark to the Virgin Islands. Philadelphia: Dorrance and Co., 1747.

Koht, Halvan. "The Origin of Seward's Plan to Purchase the Danish West Indies," American Historical Review, 50 (1945), 762-767.

Labat, Jean Baptiste. The Memoirs of Pierre Labat, 1693-1705. London: Constable and Co., 1931.

Larsen, Kay. Dansk Vestindien, 1666-1917. Copenhagen: Reitzels Forlag, 1922.

Lawaetz, Harold. Peter von Scholten. Copenhagen, 1940.

Levo, John E. Virgin Islanders. London: Hutchinson, 1934.

Lewis, Gordon K. "The U. S. Virgin Islands: Prototype of the Caribbean Tourist Economy." In: Mathews and Andic, eds. Politics and Economics in the Caribbean, 2d rev. ed. Rio Piedras: Institute of Caribbean Studies,

University of Puerto Rico, 1971.

________. The Virgin Islands: A Caribbean Lilliput. Evanston, Ill.: Northwestern University Press, 1972.

Lewisohn, Florence. St. Croix under Seven Flags. Hollywood, Fla.: Dukane Press, 1970.

Lightbourn, John. N. Lightbourn's West India Annual and Commercial Directory. St. Thomas, 1877-1923.

Lohse, Emil Valdemar. The Lutheran Church in the West Indies. St. Croix, 1887.

Marvel, Evalyn. Guide to Puerto Rico and the Virgin Islands. New York: Crown Publishers, 1961.

Marx, Robert F. Shipwrecks of the Virgin Islands (1523-1825). St. Thomas: Caribbean Research Institute, College of the Virgin Islands, 1969.

McGuire, James William. Geographic Dictionary of the Virgin Islands of the United States. (U. S. Coast and Geodetic Survey Special Publication No. 103, serial 269.) Washington, D. C.: G. P. O., 1925.

Melchior, Ariel. Souvenir of the American Virgin Islands. San Juan, 1935.

Moore, Ruth S. Arts in the Virgin Islands. Caribbean Research Institute, College of the Virgin Islands, 1967.

Morrill, W. T. and Dyke, Bennett. "A French Community on St. Thomas." Caribbean Studies, vol. 5, no. 4 (Jan., 1966) pp. 39-47.

Oldman, Oliver and Taylor, Milton. "Tax Incentives for Economic Growth in the U. S. Virgin Islands." Caribbean Studies, 10 (1970). 182-194.

O'Neill, Edward. The Rape of the American Virgins. New York: Praeger, 1972.

Oxholm, Axel H. The Virgin Islands of the United States. Charlotte Amalie, 1949.

Paiewonsky, Isidor. Jewish Historical Development in the Virgin Islands, 1665-1959. St. Thomas, 1959.

Paquin, Lyonel. Historical Sketch of the American Virgin Islands. St. Thomas: Antilles Printing Co., 1970.

Pares, Richard. War and Trade in the West Indies, 1739-1763. London: F. Case, 1963.

_______. Yankees and Creoles: The Trade between North America and the West Indies before the American Revolution. Hamden, Conn.: Anchor Books, 1968.

Parton, James. The Danish West Indies: Are we Bound in Honor to Pay for Them? Boston: Osgood and Co., 1869.

Pendelton, L. A. "Our New Possessions: the Danish West Indies," Journal of Negro History, 7 (1917).

Perkens, Dexter. The United States and the Caribbean. Rev. ed. Cambridge: Harvard University Press, 1966.

Reid, Charles F. editor. Bibliography of the Virgin Islands of the United States. New York: H. W. Wilson Co., 1941.

Reilly, William B. "Bermuda and the Lesser Antilles," Monthly Illustrator, 15 (Dec. 1897), 41-49.

Rogers, L. "Government of the Virgin Islands." American Political Science Review, 11, 1919.

St. Thomas and St. John (Municipality). Department of Education, Division of Public Libraries. Publications from the Virgin Islands, December, 1952. Charlotte Amalie, 1952.

Seaman, George. The Virgin Islands Dictionary. St. Thomas, 1968.

Shaw, Earl B. "The Chachas of St. Thomas." Scientific Monthly, 38 (Feb. 1934), 136-145.

Spingarn, Lawrence P. "Slavery in the Danish West Indies," American Scandinavian Review (Spring 1957), 35-43.

Stone, R. G. Meteorology of the Virgin Islands. New York, 1942.

Tansill, Charles C. The Purchase of the Danish West Indies. Baltimore: Johns Hopkins Press, 1932.

Taylor, Charles Edwin. An Island of the Sea: Descriptive of the Past and Present St. Thomas. St. Thomas, 1896.

________. Leaflets from the Danish West Indies. London: William Dawson and Sons, 1888.

Thorstenberg, Herman J. Chapter in the History of the Danish West India Islands. Ph. D. dissertation. Yale University, 1906.

Tooke, C. W. The Danish Colonial Fiscal System in the West Indies. Economic Association Report for 1900.

Tweedie, W. Earnest Men: Their Life and Work. London: T. Nelson, 1871.

U. S. Department of Interior. General Information Regarding the Virgin Islands of the U. S. Washington, D. C.: G. P. O.: 1932.

________. The Virgin Islands of the United States: Information Submitted to the Secretary General of the United Nations. annual. Washington, 1940.

U. S. House. 57th Congress 1st Session. Purchase of the Danish Islands. Report No. 2749, July 1, 1902.

U. S. House. Committee on Interior and Insular Affairs. Hearings to Revise the Organic Act of the Virgin Islands. Washington, D. C.: G. P. O., 1952.

U. S. Laws, Statutes, etc. Convention with Denmark for Purchase of the Danish West Indies, 1916. 39 Stat. 1706.

U. S. National Park Service. Mission 66 for Virgin Islands National Historic Site. Washington, D. C.: National Park Service, 1956.

U. S. Treaties, etc. Convention between the United States and Denmark, Cession of the Danish West Indies. U. S. Department of State, Treaty Series No. 629, 1916.

U. S. Virgin Islands Corporation. Report of Activities from Date of its Charter in April, 1934.

University of California. Bancroft Library. Danish West

Indies, manuscript collection.

Valles, Lionel. The Negro Family in St. Thomas. Ann Arbor: University of Michigan Press, 1967.

Virgin Islands of the United States. A Bibliography of the Virgin Islands of the United States. St. Thomas: G. P. O. 1922.

Virgin Islands of the United States. Department of Education. An Historical Account of the Purchase and Transfer of the Danish West Indies. St. Thomas: Department of Education, 1969.

________. Proposed Study Guide on Outstanding Virgin Islanders. St. Thomas, Department of Education, 1970.

________. Laws, Statutes, etc. Virgin Islands Rules and Regulations. 2d ed. Oxford, N. H.: Equity Pub. Co., 1970.

Walloe, August. The St. Thomas Almanak and Commerical Advertiser. St. Thomas, 1877-

Weinstein, E. A. Cultural Aspects of Delusion: A Psychiatric Study of the Virgin Islands. New York, 1962.

Westergaard, Waldemar Christian. The Danish West Indies Under Company Rule (1671-1754). New York: Macmillan Co., 1917.

Work, John C. A Short History of the Virgin Islands. St. Thomas: Carib Graphic Arts, n. d.

Zabriskie, Luther K. The Virgin Islands of the U. S. A. New York: Putnam Sons, 1918.